ACHIEVING EXCELLENCE IN YOUR DESIGN PRACTICE

ACHIEVING EXCELLENCE IN YOUR DESIGN PRACTICE

STUART W. ROSE

WHITNEY LIBRARY OF DESIGN
an imprint of Watson-Guptill Publications
New York

First published in 1987 in New York by Whitney Library of Design
an imprint of Watson-Guptill Publications
a division of Billboard Publications, Inc.
1515 Broadway, New York, NY 10036

Library of Congress Cataloging-in-Publication Data

Rose, Stuart W.
   Achieving excellence in your design practice.

   1. Architectural firms—United States—Management.
2. Architectural services marketing—United States.
3. Engineering firms—United States—Management.
4. Engineering services marketing—United States.
5. Design services—United States—Marketing.
I. Title.
NA1996.R58   1987   720'.68   87-6113
ISBN 0-8230-7005-0

Distributed in the United Kingdom by Phaidon Press Ltd.
Littlegate House, St. Ebbe's St., Oxford

Manufactured in the U.S.A.

First printing, 1987

1 2 3 4 5 6 7 8 9 / 93 92 91 90 89 88 87

Senior Editor: Julia Moore
Associate Editor: Victoria Craven-Cohn
Designer: Areta Buk
Production Manager: Ellen Greene
Set in 11-point Baskerville

CONTENTS

PREFACE

"Being eminently good"—a dictionary definition of excellence—is more important than anything else to most design professionals.

It is cherished at least as much as fame.

It is usually valued more than financial success.

The design professions don't have an exclusive claim on excellence as a totem. In 1968, John W. Gardner confronted the American education systems with his book *Excellence*. Since then the notion of being eminently good has been a hallowed one.

It leapt from the world of education to the community of corporate management in 1982, when Thomas J. Peters and Robert H. Waterman Jr. published *In Search of Excellence: Lessons from America's Best-Run Companies*. Peters' and Waterman's ideas and observations on excellence were quickly mainstreamed as concrete principles and practices of good management.

Design professionals, however, still regard excellence in idealistic terms, which is different from the concrete, results-oriented ways that most professional and business people regard it. Also, most design professionals—which includes architects, interior designers, consulting engineers, landscape architects, and graphic designers—work in organizations that are *radically* different from America's "best-run" companies.

The goal of this book is to show *how* design firms are different from other professional and business organizations.

And to provide *concrete methods* that professional design firms can *use* to achieve excellence.

CHAPTER 1

HOW DESIGN FIRMS ARE UNIQUE

Design professionals think of their work situations as unique. In some ways they are. And in some ways they are not.

The design professions are unique from the standpoint of history—the events that bred the professions' culture and norms.

Design professionals are unique in possessing certain traits that are common to their subculture but are not common to other professional groups.

Design professionals are not unique in that they do have *organizational systems*. Organizational theory describes holistic models into which anybody's organization can fit, *including* those of design professionals.

This chapter has four themes, which are treated in four sections.

The first section looks at some formative experiences and natural preferences shared by most design professionals.

The second section examines the "situation"—the norms of organization that exist within the design professions.

The third section is about the personal styles of the design professional. Certain behavioral qualities have powerful implications for how firms are managed. Design professionals tend to have distinctive behavioral styles. These styles are part of the reason why we became design professionals, as opposed to corporate middle managers or just managers.

The final section looks at organizational systems in terms of holistic systems or models and shows how and why design firms, as organizations, fit within the major model types.

Self-awareness will come from looking at our profession in these structured contexts and having this self-awareness can start you down a path of change toward greater excellence in your firm.

Formative Experiences and Natural Preferences

Let's begin with an objective look at ourselves, especially:

- How we entered into the design profession
- Things we tend to like or not like

In early architectural education, the Ecole des Beaux Arts, in Paris, was a potent model. The school was structured around its professors, each of whom was an artist. When you went to the university then, you studied, or essentially, you apprenticed under a particular artist. That professor had a studio, or an atelier. The same thing occurred around Rembrandt and around Michelangelo. This is the atelier system.

Many professionals today want to start their careers with certain firms—typically those keyed to a leader in the firm—to learn how a great architect or designer works. Certain engineering firms have unique capabilities, and many beginning engineers want to work with those firms, at least for a one- or two-year learning period. You can call it a form of hero worship, if you like. But it goes back to the notion of the atelier. And that the person in that "studio" possesses a tremendous professional strength or expertise.

A typical way in which many firms begin is this: A new professional goes to work in another firm (atelier) for one to three to five years. A base of experience develops as the professional accumulates several-year periods of experience in two or three different firms. At that point in the advancing professional's life, if the firm he or she is with does not provide a clear career track through which to become an associate, junior partner, or partner (an owner in the firm), the professional leaves and starts his or her own firm.

This happens in medicine and law, in accounting and design.

Now we have, let's say, an architect who opens his own firm, Arthur J. Freen Associates. Initially the firm *is* Arthur J. Freen (the associates don't exist). Later he brings in a part-time bookkeeper or a part-time secretary. And when Freen has some success, he hires a drafter, and then a junior designer.

Gradually, a network of people who like to study under Freen is formed. And "Atelier Freen" is born. Over time, the people in the firm become an extension of Freen—it's his atelier. If staff members need to express their own identity, they may need to leave Freen's organization.

In summary, these are the initial preconditions that contribute to the unique makeup of the design firm:

- It is not an *organization* that's been formed to practice engineering or architecture or interior design
- It is a *person* who starts off to practice his or her art
- And that person begins adding staff to extend himself or herself, in order to work more effectively

Business management consultant, Peter Piven, FAIA, and his colleague, Weld Coxe, have developed a concept that perceives some design firms as "practice-based businesses," and others as "business-based practices." Most design professionals have business-based practices. More than anything in the world, we want to do our architecture, our interiors, our graphics, our engineering. The "business" aspect of our profession is often viewed as a necessary irritant, if not an evil.

> In order to do a project, you have to have a client. And to get a client, you have to (ugh) market. And, in order to pay for everything, you have to (yuk) negotiate fees.

This preference for practice over business dominates in as many as 95 percent of all design firms. So the logical extension of this is that management concepts and methods need to make *minimal* energy demands on the design professional.

More importantly, everything being managed must be framed in a context that leads primarily to the purpose of conducting a better *practice*, not building a better business—at least not for the sake of building a better business.

Design professionals, are usually not trained as managers.

And we don't really *want* the training. We'll enthusiastically attend courses to develop technical expertise but reluctantly sign up for courses that provide ideas about building better businesses.

This observation is not intended to be a negative one.

What it means is that—given our druthers—we'd rather put our energy into practice issues, not on running a business.

Norms of Design Professions

Every professional group establishes, through history, certain business norms, among them:

- Sizes of firms
- Working relationships between firms and clients
- Relationships between firms
- Position in the marketplace

Most design firms are *small*. Ninety percent have eight people or fewer (or ten or less, depending on which survey you look at).

The typical firm has four people or six people or ten people.

More of a *family*.

A group that can sit in one room within, say, 15 feet of one another.

Even some of the largest design firms—firms of 1,500, 2,000, or 3,000—are really made up of 40 offices with, perhaps, 150 as a maximum number in any one office. And within that office there can be departments of 15 or 20 people.

Design firms provide services.

We sell our *time*, not widgets.

When you have a widget, you can *demonstrate* it. An organization that produces widgets can have people committed to design, to production, and to a variety of tasks. In a collective way, they can produce and sell the widgets and have a profitable business. And they can feel good about their product.

With our service, *we* are the product. We deal in "trust relationships" significantly more than do some other professionals. Personal integrity and technical knowledge—and the "right" situation—is often the total of what a client hires.

Furthermore, our service is a reflection of a particular *art*. Typically, everyone in our firm is personally committed to the art—even people who are not technically practicing it, such as marketing professionals or support staff. They often work for less money than they can make in other professions because they really enjoy being "near the artist." They relate personally to the *mission*, partly because in the atelier environment the mission takes on a highly personal quality.

Another distinctive quality of the design professional's situation is the major separation that often occurs between those who are our clients and those who are the beneficiaries or users of our services.

> In medicine, your doctor decides whether to have your tonsils or appendix removed. The service is provided for your benefit by the practitioner of your own choosing. It's *direct*.

Many design professionals work for developers, who are the clients and who dictate what will happen in a project. A design firm must be keenly responsive to the developer/client. But the developer is going to lease or sell that project to someone else, who will be the real user. It could be renters in an apartment complex or merchants in a shopping mall.

So one of our norms is that we often have *two* marketplaces or *two* clients to whom we must respond, but only one of whom is paying us directly. The separation between the two—client and end-user—can be dramatic.

Designers tend to design to accommodate the actual users. Where this happens regularly, firms will usually experience problems in the marketplace, because meeting the users' needs tends to make firms less responsive to the clients. The reverse also occurs.

Some firms arrange dual, parallel structures to achieve a synergistic "win-win" result. Some people in these firms are client-oriented; others in the same firms focus on their disciplines, which tend to be user-oriented. And the gap is managed internally. Those firms, alas, are rare.

Relationships between design firms, the third category of our business norms, are characterized by complex linkages.

The successful completion of most projects requires input from a variety of disciplines or arts. In fact, a huge range of design professionals may be called on for a specific project, and these may be drawn from different firms.

With each firm having a high commitment to its art and its own working style—remember, the atelier system encourages a firm to become a personal extension of the leader—real cultural gaps develop between firms. These clashes of cultures, heightened when a huge number of small firms have to work together, are real obstacles to excellence and need to be addressed.

The final business norm is a fallacy, not a fact.

> It is: The low bid wins.

Many design firms behave as if clients are only looking for the best price.

Design professionals tend to be intimidated by potential clients fairly easily. This may be more true for architects and interior designers than for engineers. Aesthetics judging is quite subjective. Design professionals often do not to put as high a premium on their uniqueness and *value* as they should.

One of the squeezing tactics clients often use—to their advantage—is "I can get it cheaper down the street."

Because we intimidate fairly easily, we tend to *believe* this. We offer and counteroffer. In effect, we negotiate against ourselves.

The two-edged sword of our marketplace position has these two sides:

- Our belief that the lowest pricer *is* the winner
- Our timidity (born of uncertain self-value) over calling the lowest-price bluff

When we look at the unique qualities that are our strengths—and realize that the client cannot buy them down the street—then we have a better bargaining position.

Personal Styles of Design Professionals

Many behavioral models can be used to describe personal styles. Design professionals vary within the range described by these models.

However, some style traits do tend to dominate and these qualities distinguish us, significantly, from other groups. In fact, many of these traits *caused* us to choose a design profession.

One of the reasons for clashes of cultures, which was just described as a norm in relationships between firms, is that every design professional comes from a particular discipline. Further, each discipline has several areas within which to focus. Not only would a civil engineer, for example, come out of "civil," but he or she is likely to be specialized in hydrology, in wastewater management, or in water resources.

One of the problems that specialization precipitates is a lack of *holistic* perspective. Many of us call ourselves problem-solvers, but we often look only at the problems as defined within our discipline.

Architects talk about architectural problems.

Interior designers talk about interior design problems.

Engineers talk about engineering or geotechnical problems.

In fact, what our client experiences is "a problem."

The solution may require the services of *several* disciplines.

Physicians share some of the same thinking. Orthopedic surgeons tend to think only in terms of bones. Generally, only holistic physicians look at the whole body (or person) rather than at the symptoms.

The physician analogy—treating symptoms and not working backwards to the holistic cause—is similar to our problem. We often expect our clients to have their problems "packaged" in *our* terms.

Many of us are more comfortable working with what we call "an educated client," who "understands what he needs." That means he or she can translate his or her needs into terminology that *we* understand.

For example, rather than the architect asking, "*Why* do you need a building?" (because, perhaps, renovating the existing building is an adequate solution. Or, perhaps, the client is looking at the building as a form of investment), we expect our client to say, "I need a three-story building."

When the client doesn't say what he or she needs, the architect may ask, "How many stories would you like your building to have?"

The client may not *know*. Yet, when we pose those kinds of questions, we are obliging our clients to make problem-solving decisions about the number of floors, the square footage, number of windows, and countless other things. In short, we stay very close to our discipline-training boundaries and typically abdicate our roles as holistic problem-solvers.

We can learn a lot about our limitations and styles from looking at behavior models.

One particularly light-shedding model, developed by Richard E. Byrd, Ph.D., a Minneapolis-based management consultant, measures two behavioral dimensions: creativity and risk-taking.

Byrd developed a matrix using those two behaviors as dimensions. And he defined eight personal styles within that matrix, which he calls the "Creatrix."

The four corner styles are the extremes. Most of us fall into one of the four center styles, which are more balanced. Briefly, here are characterizations of the eight styles:

The Reproducer is someone who simply repeats over and over and over. He or she takes *no* risks. Many firms need Reproducers, people who can do the job consistently, over and over again and, in fact, with some enthusiasm. Most of us cannot do that. The Reproducer is a fairly rare type.

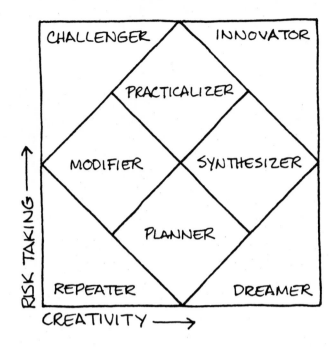

Another corner style, one high on risk-taking, is the Challenger. This person takes risks but hasn't ideas of his or her own to develop. Because Challengers do not generate ideas, they also don't recognize ideas of other people in the firm. Challengers typically pound their fists on the table and tell everybody else why their ideas are valueless, which has the effect of burying good ideas. Challengers have a value in questioning entrenched practices. They help the process of discarding activities that are no longer productive.

In a third corner, high on creativity, but low on risk-taking, is the Dreamer. Dreamers have a *lot* of ideas. But they lack the courage to put those ideas to work.

The fourth type, high on risk-taking and high on creativity, is the Innovator. This person *always* has a new idea and will always be willing to lay everything on the line for that idea. And if the Innovator does not receive support for the idea, he or she may quit the firm. Innovators often fail and are typically not well liked. Innovators are used to losing. However, they can lead us to those periodic breakthroughs that have huge impacts on our firms—or our society—for years afterward. Buckminster Fuller is an example of a Design Innovator; he had scores of ideas that went nowhere, but a few of major impact.

Among the four central styles, the Modifier is one who takes ideas that have been developed and implemented by others in the firm and updates or refines them. The Modifier is a moderate risk-taker with a little creativity. A

Modifier keeps things up-to-date. A production process in the firm may begin by adopting variations—not big changes, but variations.

A Planner has little risk-taking capacity and is moderately creative. This person has many ideas and an ability to implement the more practical ones. City planners, for instance, make a lot of plans. But, because their plans are constantly subject to change, they learn to stay "flexible." Planners are good at setting annual plans, three-year plans, five-year plans. They offer ideas. They will give commitment to the ideas. And they're not very rigid.

The Practicalizer is a reasonably high risk-taker. With somewhat more creativity than the Challenger, the Practicalizer can understand ideas generated by a Dreamer or an Innovator. Very often, in fact, it's the Practicalizer who takes the more creative people's ideas and uses his or her risk-taking ability to put them to *use*. Practicalizers may be very "political," when politics is defined as the art of the possible. But they may "sell out" the breakthrough ideas of the Innovator when resistance builds.

The eighth style is the Synthesizer, a type characterized by high creativity and moderate risk-taking. A Synthesizer can take ideas from one place and another and pull them together. And because of a reasonable risk-taking capacity, the Synthesizer can put reasonable, good ideas into action. What the Synthesizer lacks, however, is enough risk-taking capacity to work with extreme ideas.

Practicalizers and Synthesizers typically make better managers than other types identified by Byrd's Creatrix because they are able to relate to the norms of their profession yet cause some action.

> The design professions do not seem to have as much risk-taking capacity as do some other segments of our population.

As we pass through our cities, we don't see evidence of innovation implementation. We don't see the equivalent of space shuttles—or of designers with the equivalent daring it takes to sit in rockets and go into space.

Many design professionals are not willing to fight City Hall, to challenge code officials, to show fire safety officials a new way, even though they *know* their designs are safe, even though they *know* the performance of their project is well above what's required.

If "it isn't stated that way," we're not willing to fight for it.

Examples include the relatively unimaginative uses of prefabrication. Airplanes are put together to the thousandth of an inch. The technology exists, as Buckminster Fuller and Carl Koch realized years ago.

The lag reflects our lower risk-taking qualities, which suggests that we have a higher number of Dreamers, Planners, and Synthesizers.

The reason these styles are significant to us is that change in design firms probably *cannot* be very radical, given the fact that few of us are Innovators, Challengers, or Practicalizers.

> For most of us, ideas for change need to be "reasonable" or "pragmatic" to be acceptable. The instinct to go for the big breakthrough does not come naturally to us.

Another behavioral model, known as the Myers Briggs Type Indicator (MBTI), published originally in the *Myers Briggs Type Indicator Manual* by Isabel Briggs Meyers in 1962, measures four behavioral phenomena, each with polar paired opposites. On each of the four continuums, a person can be near 50–50, heavy to one side, or heavy to the other by varying degrees.

One of these four pairs is known as Judging and Perceiving.

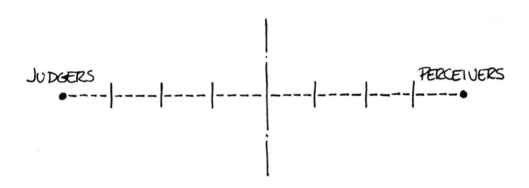

In the terms of this model, a Judger is someone who evaluates and makes decisions. This person gathers the information necessary to solve a problem, pulls it together, and solves the problem.

Judgers tend to be very focused on producing answers. Someone who is an extreme Judger may come up with answers too quickly, before there has been time to gather adequate information.

Perceivers, on the other hand, enjoy perceiving. They don't like bringing an end to the fact-gathering process. They want to continue to gather more data, and more data, and more data.

New data, they are sure, leads to new perceptions.

Both types, essentially, are needed. We do need to gather information. And we do need to make decisions.

As a rule, design professionals seem to be more dominated by Judgers. Our focus tends to be more on the project than on the client.

At the American Institute of Architects headquarters, a small group of clients were invited to talk about some of their perceptions and needs in relation to architects. It was an ideal opportunity to gather market research information. At one point, they were asked to cite problems that architects consistently presented to them. One of the most dominant sounded like this:

> "When they finish a job, it's the last you ever see of them . . .
> until seven years later when another job comes up! Somehow,
> magically, they seem to perceive that the next job is there. And
> suddenly, they appear with their new brochure in hand!"

That behavior reflects a Judger-dominated style:

- Focus on the project
- Do the project
- Go on to another project and another client

However, a building may soon need a roof inspection. Or, one year after completion, the carpeting may not have been cleaned properly; neither the architect nor the interior designer—who are off doing their next project— are doing periodic inspections to discover that the cleaning crew simply did not know what solvent to use.

And the building's owner? The owner is angry.

The design professional in this project was not continuing to care for the client on a month-by-month, day-to-day basis, even under contract.

Perceivers are better oriented toward *long-term* relationships. However, an extreme Perceiver may never get down to the real work of analyzing a *specific* project and solving its problems.

> A balance between judging and perceiving behaviors is needed
> to achieve excellence: problem-solving on projects and also
> continuing client and project-management programs.

Facilities management is a service that's catching on. It's a form of continuous service, with monthly or annual retainer fees to look after a project. Engineering firms call it "O&M," operations and maintenance. It's a dynamite approach, if firms can find Perceivers to *implement* it.

A second set of behavioral-style paired opposites described in the Myers Briggs Type Indicator is Sensing and Intuiting, with the extremes of each behavior appearing at the extreme ends of the scale.

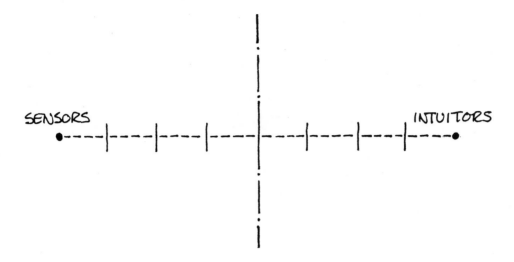

SENSORS   INTUITORS

The design professions, by definition, address the physical sciences—geo-technical engineering, mechanical engineering, architecture, interior design. We all deal with feet and inches, numbers of stories, and so many MGD (millions of gallons per day). And we tend to think in "fact" or in "sensing" terms.

Intuitors tend to read between the lines. They look more for *possibilities*. Rather than seeing the facts presented, they see what the facts could lead to.

Both qualities are useful.

While design professionals tend to think of themselves more as Intuitors, we seem, in fact, largely to be Sensors. Certain marketing training programs, such as the Mandeville Techniques, teach diagnostics. In this diagnostic approach, people are helped to look more at the client's feelings and concerns and at some of the subtle, "between-the-lines" data. Most design professionals have to struggle to develop that capability. We tend to be oriented—especially after we've been doing it for 20 or 30 years—to getting the facts and going to work on the solution.

> Excellent organizations tend to value the *intuitive* over the intellectual: reading between the lines, making guesses, and working hunches.

One final behavioral style that impacts on design professionals is one that relates to learning: *how* we assimilate knowledge. We tend to communicate with others in the same style in which we learn. If we tend to learn in terms of conceptual models, we tend to communicate our ideas to others with conceptual frameworks.

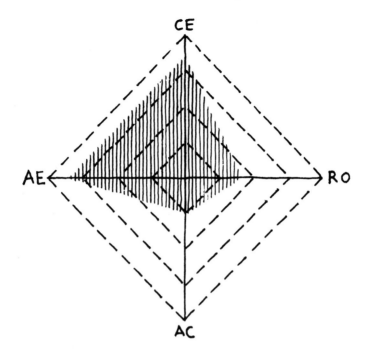

This particular learning model has four parts.

The first is Concrete Experience (CE), learning by doing.

> I learn it by *doing* it. You hold my hand. Take me through the process a step at a time. I'm doing it, but under your guidance.

The second learning style is Reflective Observation (RO).

> You do it. Let me watch you. And, as I watch you, I'll begin to understand the phenomenon and can then do it myself.

Many people learn about construction by observing construction workers. They are Reflective Observers. In meetings, certain people never jump into the dialogue early on. They observe and reflect. Later, however, they'll often share their observations. Sometimes, in fact, they have keen insights.

The third learning style is Abstract Conceptualization (AC).

> Just give me the concept. I'll be able to use it directly.

The purest example is the math professor who loves to develop the "general formula." In contrast, design professionals often come through math in "plug and shove" fashion: The instructor provides a formula for determining stress in a certain beam. We plug in the specifics for the given beam.

Behold, out comes the solution. (The response is *not* an abstract conceptualizer's response.)

If we are asked to derive the formula for defining stress on a beam, we'd say, "That's not my kind of thing. That's for the theorists."

Abstract Conceptualizers can learn directly from theories. They like to be presented with a concept. They can see where that concept would apply. And then they apply it.

The fourth learning style is Active Experimentation (AE). Experimenters are similar to the Concrete Experience types in that they too are doers. However, Active Experimenters *don't* like the structure. They don't want their hands held. They prefer to reinvent the wheel, because they believe they may discover a new twist in the process.

The design professionals are equally represented by all of these styles. However, in the United States, our learning systems tend to favor the Abstract Conceptualizers. Most of our exams are of the recite and regurgitate sort.

Design professionals *do* enroll in studio courses, including laboratories, design studios, problem-solving studios, soils laboratories, and field testing. Learning this way is more experiential than conceptual.

> Overall, design professionals tend to favor doing (CE) and experimenting (AE) learning styles. Our clustering is shown by the shaded area of the diagram.

Incidentally, the four styles complement one another. For instance:

> Someone can take me by the hand through a new process, such as how to work on a CADD system. I can *observe* what happens and *reflect* on the results. I can develop the *concepts* about what's happening inside the CADD system. And, when I'm left alone, I can sit down and play with it on my own. I can begin to *experiment*.

The point of entry into the cycle can vary, depending on our personal bias. The greater the orientation toward *doing*, however, the more we're likely to cause excellence-building changes in our firms.

The System May Not Be the Solution

Inasmuch as we've just suggested that design professionals, as a group, may not be heavy Abstract Conceptualizers, let's move immediately to providing some concepts, some frameworks of organization.

Many organizational theories, or models, exist. Most management consultants have one or two or three favorites.

Models of organizations can be seen as different windows looking on the same garden. Each offers a different perspective. Each explains that organization in a different light.

Models present a clear picture of some phenomena and explain how our design firms can become more successful—more *excellent* than they are now:

- A model can add clarity to the way we see ourselves
- A model can explain why we've had particular successes doing things one way and failures doing things another way
- Models provide guidelines for *change*

A management consultant named Rensis Likert developed a model of organizations that is defined by four systems and published these models in his book, *The Human Organization: Its Management and Value* in 1962. Essentially, each system is defined by *how decisions are made* within the firm. In System One, the decision-making rule is:

> I'm the principal of the firm. I make the decision, using my best judgment. And I may or may not announce that decision, depending on the sensitivity of the subject. I'll decide what to share, also.

Likert calls that the Autocratic system.

Autocratic systems tend to work reasonably quickly. They have consistency—just one source of decisions. And control is clear.

The negative side of the Autocratic system is low morale. Everyone in a firm, except the decision-maker, feels like a second, third, or fourth-class citizen. Some cat-and-mouse games tend to exist. Confusion abounds when the principal does not share information.

An Autocratic system comes very naturally in design firms that are ateliers.

The decision-making rule in System Two is:

> I make a decision. Then I try to sell my ideas to the others. For example, I say to them, "I set a budget of $180,000 for this project. I've negotiated the best fee I could. I've taken profit off that fee to maintain the firm's profitability. We have to be able to do the job at $180,000. What do you guys think?"
>
> The point is, the budget is not extremely negotiable. But I'm going to try to convince my staff of the wisdom—or at least reasonableness—of my thinking.

System Two is called Benevolent Autocratic.

The fact is, the decision has been made *before* the ideas are "sold."

In most firms, the ideas are not terrible or unreasonable; the principal usually has had more experience. The issue is usually not the quality of the ideas as much as how staff people react to them. The strength in Likert's System Two is its focus on the leader. More decision time is required than in an Autocratic system, because the leader has to take time to talk to people. The tradeoff is that morale is slightly higher. More people know what is happening in the firm. And because the principal shares information, staff members feel more personally appreciated.

The rule in System Three is:

> I will make the decision. However, *before* I do, I will ask staff people their opinions, maybe very extensively. After I have their opinions, I will go back to my office and make a decision. I still have the authority or power.

The System Three model is known as Consultative.

In Consultative systems, the staff does have more *ownership* in ideas that happen. Principals still make the decisions. But if they really listen, they can gain from possibly significant contributions by others. A young designer recently out of college hasn't been ground into mediocrity by fighting building codes for 23 years. That young designer may have a fresh insight. The negative side of the Consultative system is the amount of patience required. The principal may not feel as though there is quite as much control. And it generally takes longer.

> In a firm of 100 people, it may not be possible to talk with everyone. The rule, generally, is: Consult with all people who are *directly* affected by the issue.

The successful Japanese management systems, as described by William Ouchi in *Theory Z*, are largely consultative. If we, in design firms, are to learn from them, we need to be conscious of some Western cultural conditioning that makes Consultative management difficult to implement:

- Our reluctance to invest in *time* cost (though the Japanese find that implementation time is drastically less when everyone buys into the solution)
- A principal who likes to make decisions and "get on with business" may feel impotent
- Strong designers tend to be short on patience
- Many design professionals believe that the group process is a dysfunctional way to make decisions

The trick to achieving success through consultative management is to develop skills for achieving quality ideas, quickly, from a group of people. It *is* doable. But training is needed to learn those skills.

The rule in System Four is:

> *We* will make the decision.
>
> If I'm a principal of the firm, I'm part of the "we." If I veto an idea, it's still vetoed. However, a junior drafter can *also* veto it.

The name for System Four is Participatory, and it *is* fully participatory. It is not a popular model.

The benefit of System Four is that it produces the *highest* morale. In a sense, everybody in the firm is a principal. All feel as though they're contributing. In fact, they all are contributing.

Tremendous commitment and intensity of achievement exists. The Participatory model has the same time costs as the Consultative model—in fact, to an even greater degree. The principal often fears that he or she has given away the store. That fear can be resolved through the use of critical group decision-making skills. And it helps when principals understand that they never have to support a "no" decision.

Likert appears to have a bias toward System Four and away from System One. A lot of his work was done in the 1960s, when participatory management was touted as the answer to everything. A few happy corporations did evolve as participatory models. But they were not necessarily profitable.

> Most design firms, from tests and observation, are System *Two* cultures. Some are split between Systems One and Two, some between Two and Three. And firms vary according to the issue. In some aspects, such as design development, we may be much more Consultative. In finance, we may be much more Autocratic and close to the vest.
>
> Our preference for System Two, Benevolent Autocratic, is consistent with our atelier origins. We've hooked up with a star.

System Two can be successful. What principals must do, in every case, is to ask which system makes them most *comfortable*. If you're most comfortable with System One—and not as effective outside of it—you simply make that clear to people as they join your firm and buy into your culture. If they are not comfortable with your culture, then they should work elsewhere.

If, as the principal of a firm, you're not comfortable with your firm's culture, you'll need to shift it. But know that shifting a culture is going to demand a lot of work. Many firms shift from System Two to Three, for instance. Even with training and periodic coaching, habits are so deeply entrenched that change—while possible—is difficult.

Another organizational model, developed by Byrd, refers to "relational" and "rational" styles of organization.

The two qualities are structured as polar extremes.

> For the "rational" model, the motto might be: "The system is the solution."

A rational type of organization would have clearly defined organization charts that describe the system. The functions of the organizations are described in boxes.

Within each function is a person. The person has a job description that details what needs to be done to carry out the function. When each function is being performed, the organization "works"—much as a smooth-running machine needs all of its parts working properly.

If the firm has problems—a recession hits, or several key projects are lost to competitors, or profits are down—principals return to the chart, to "the system." And they take out their screwdrivers, so to speak, and make changes in the system to correct the problem.

The benefits of a rational system include clarity. Everybody understands what has to happen. And they do what is needed. The system tends to hinge less on whether or not I like you than on whether you're good at your function and I'm good at my function.

If the marketing department is responsible for developing a client contact with a technical person, they do it. Their personal styles may not be compatible, given their orientations. But because those are their two roles in the system, they will perform them, and perform them *well*.

> A rational system is also less vulnerable to changes of heroes.

In a long-established, reputable firm in Kansas, the principal had built all the personal contacts. The firm was like an atelier. It was a quality firm with a talented and committed staff. The principal died a few years ago. And the firm has been coasting ever since, close to the edge of going under.

They have skills and confidence, but both were built on the personality and the relationships established by that one person.

That firm was *not* a rational system. A rational system is more like a machine. If one person leaves, somebody else can be inserted to fill that job, and knowledge of that fact can lower morale.

A "machine" can be run humanely. IBM's example of promoting from within, investing in extensive job training and staff development, and performing responsible out-placement when an employee and job can't be made to fit, has been an outstanding example of a humane rational system.

At the other extreme is the *relational* firm.

> For such a firm, the motto would probably be: "We are as good as our best people."

An example of a relational organization is your family. Even if your teen-ager doesn't seem to fit in the family, you don't throw the kid out on the street. The *person* comes first. Likewise, many small firms, and most larger firms, will carry deadwood.

For example, a senior vice president who has been with the firm for years begins drinking heavily under the pressure from the job. But he will not be fired. The person has been valuable to the firm. He has useful skills. And he has been there a long time. The feeling is, "He's paid his dues, and he's a good friend. We *can't* throw him out."

> A relational firm exhibits a lot of caring.

In our profession a firm of six is like a small family. If someone comes into the firm and doesn't do some part of the job well, we will tend to find some other things for him or her to do that better utilizes his or her talents and abilities.

Byrd once administered a "systems" test at a large conference of consulting engineers. Roughly 125 engineers answered 25 questions, each with two alternative answers—one relational and one rational.

After Byrd presented the relational-rational model to them, he decoded the test and asked how many of the engineers had given a predominance of relational answers. A sea of hands went up—virtually the entire room. Only two or three had given a preponderance of rational answers.

Japanese organizations typically are relational. That's why they spend time together outside of work, at picnics or at other recreational or social activities. When people right out of school go to work in a Japanese firm, they are basically committing themselves until they are 55 years old. They *really* make a career decision.

Probably 95 to 98 percent of all design firms—whether they're 1,400-person firms or 100-person firms or 6-person firms—seem to be relational.

Relational firms typically have no job descriptions or organization chart. Clarity comes from constant communication, from elbow-rubbing. It's a process of sitting down with somebody over a cup of coffee, beginning to *know* the person, reading between the lines, and talking about what's happening in the office.

Rational firms, by contrast, run well with management-by-objectives (MBO), the unambiguous stating of clear, measurable objectives. With goals stated, people can discuss how they're going to achieve the results, what resources will be needed, and how they'll evaluate the results.

A 500-person engineering firm in California hired a management consultant to install an MBO system in their thoroughly relational firm. He tried. After a lot of pain and a lot of dollars—in both fees and downtime—they finally discarded it.

The consultant didn't understand the nature of the firm's culture and that MBO, which can be very effective in rational cultures, can be destructive in relational cultures. Goals can be set in relational firms, but only through long dialogues that produce "understanding."

For us, in short, the system may *not* be the solution.

Again referring to Byrd's work, he has described, in another model, two aspects of firms. The first is the *production* side.

We have a project. We have a certain technical capability. And our job is to execute the project on time, within budget, with care, with quality control, and with a certain amount of creativity. That's how we earn our paychecks and pay our bills. However, when some *new* technology needs to be developed and introduced in a firm, the production model often is inappropriate.

Research and Development (R&D) is typically an overhead activity. It has a lot of risks. Many people in the firm may not favor a particular R&D project.

Byrd suggested what he called a "collateral system." The process works *parallel* with the rest of the firm. The collateral system tends to be organized by committees or task groups. The groups often are not hierarchical. And the groups are all *temporary*.

Many collateral groups are looking at CADD, looking for answers to questions like, "Where do we do the research?" "How do we decide what CADD system to buy and what software to use?" "How do we handle the training?"

That is a perfect example of a project that *should* be a collateral activity. Getting the answers might involve a certain amount of downtime; or the committee could meet in the evenings or during lunch hours. Once the CADD system is installed and people in the firm are trained, the committee must *go out of existence*.

The CADD system then becomes part of the production side of the firm—also known as the "cash cow," because it pays our bills and our salaries.

Most design firms don't recognize and, therefore, don't form a regular collateral system. Large corporations may have R&D departments. Design firms usually don't. But in order to *improve* the level of performance, to introduce new technologies, new disciplines, new equipment, new production techniques, new quality control systems—we, too, need a well-tended collateral system.

> Collateral is a separate system that causes improvement and greater excellence of our firms.

BSW Architects in Tulsa was, at the time this took place, a three-to-five-person firm led by Charles "Chief" Boyd and his partner, who led the programming development of a lot of CADD software. Boyd is entrepreneurial and figured out ways to apply the software. BSW Architects merged with another firm that had about seven people. They had good contacts and a quality design reputation, but they didn't have the CADD system. Within a few months of the merger they had more than 30 people. Students coming out of school were giving their eye teeth to work there. The firm had first choice of new talent because they were at the edge of their technology. And clients sensed the special quality of their firm.

The business snowballed.

How did it happen? The firm took a risk, and they exploited the collateral possibilities at hand.

> Collateral activity in a firm keeps it healthy and gives it freshness and vigor.

In the chapters ahead, we'll refer to the discussions of preferences, styles, professional norms, and organizational models just introduced. They will be like roadsigns—along the journey to recognizing and achieving excellence in your design practice.

CHAPTER 2

ACTION ORIENTATION

One of the qualities successful design firms have in common with each other is action orientation—the preference for doing over not doing. Thomas J. Peters and Robert H. Waterman Jr. found this quality in all of the "excellent" corporations and organizations they studied in researching *In Search of Excellence*. They called it "a bias for action."

Action orientation in a firm is precipitated by six key conditions:

- Fluidity
- Sidestreaming
- Experimentation
- Lots of experiments
- Low-cost experiments
- An *environment* for experimentation

This chapter looks at these six conditions and provides examples of excellent design firms that—consciously or unconsciously—have made some or all these six qualities part of their organizational dynamics.

Action orientation is very basic. It underlies at least three other tenets of excellence, which are the subjects of Chapters 3, 4, and 5 of this book: (1) closeness to your clients, (2) entrepreneurial spirit, and (3) investment in your people.

Fluidity

The first quality needed to precipitate action is fluidity, which is defined as people knowing people in a casual, elbow-rubbing way. This guideline goes back to the relational concept of firms discussed in the previous chapter.

As you'd imagine, in a corporation with 20,000 or 120,000 employees, having people at the top visit the people at the bottom is difficult. Yet many of the great executives do exactly that.

In O'Brien-Gere Engineering, a firm of over 300 in Syracuse, New York, the chairman of the board made a personal resolution: "At least once a week, I'm going to have a brown bag lunch."

He decided that on one of the five days he would have no committee meetings or business meetings. He would instead go out on the floor, look for an employee who was also brown bagging, and sit down and join him or her for lunch. His goal was to get to know the employees. He did a lot of listening and learned the employees' viewpoints about what was happening in the firm.

Over a period of time, he began to build relationships with a large number of people in the organization, at all levels. He wanted to be guided by their perceptions and feelings. Listening to their ideas provided him with a broader perspective.

This executive was maintaining a personal sensitivity to the viewpoints of his employees, and because of this was better able to represent both his firm and his staff.

Brown and Caldwell, a West Coast engineering firm of over 500 people, was founded by two principals. Until his death, all incoming employees were *personally* interviewed and introduced into the firm by David Caldwell. In talking with staff, many of whom are now professional engineers, full-time marketing or management people, and project managers, most still fondly remember the initial contact and greeting and the discussions they had with a founder of their firm.

The process also enabled Caldwell to maintain his perspective about the needs and interests of new junior employees. The knowledge led to more successful planning and action in the firm.

Richard Marshall, a San Francisco architect with a small firm, took a marketing course that involved diagnostics, a structured process for listening to client concerns. (Specifically, this was the Mandeville Techniques process taught under the sponsorship of AIA, ACEC, NSPE, ASLA, ASID, and other professional societies, and now used by over 14,000 design professionals.)

Marshall quickly experienced the marketing success, as he won a consistent flow of new contracts. Then he began thinking.

> "Maybe it wouldn't be such a bad idea to use this same process—which leads to better relationships and understanding—with my employees!"

Marshall had a seven-person firm, including himself, a secretary, and five other architectural staff people with various degrees of experience. He took his staff to lunch, individually, and at regular intervals. He might, for instance, take one staff member to lunch every two weeks. Of every ten lunches, one was with an employee. Approximately four times a year, each employee had lunch with the principal.

The lunch would be casual, not formal. It wasn't connected with appraisal. And, again, Marshall was mostly listening. He essentially applied the Mandeville Techniques process to his staff. The improved employee relationships reduced turnover and improved morale in the firm.

In a one-person firm, dialogue with colleagues can be fruitful in helping a sole proprietor to crystalize directions for action.

In a two-person firm, have lunch periodically to discuss goals and direction.

If you have two partners and a secretary, the three of you (or five or ten) should go to lunch once a month. Just talk generally about how things are going and where you are headed.

Hold these dialogues away from your day-to-day environment. If not lunch, try a Saturday morning meeting at a site away from your office, where the symbols of daily demands are absent.

> Fluidity adapted to each firm size—seems to produce *consistent* payoff.

The best approach to precipitating a continuing flow of new activity is through temporary subgroups. Each subgroup has a particular task, or purpose, for its existence. When the purpose is fulfilled, the subgroup goes out of existence.

Standing committees, such as a management committee, become regular "institutionalized" parts of a firm. Once any group develops a relatively permanent status, an attitude of "if it doesn't happen now, it'll happen later" takes over. Action slows.

Here, we're talking about your firm having a particular problem, such as better project management or automation. Form a small task group to do something about it. The "group" could be one person, if that's the only person who cares about the problem. The group could have two people or four people to work on the problem. After a while, they are to come up with some resolution to that problem.

The task group's time for achievement would probably be three or four months maximum. Preferably, your task group should lead you to some action in the first two or three weeks.

The group could come to work early or have lunch together, or stay late once or twice a week. With a little off-hours work, they should begin to come up with some solutions and actions within just a few weeks.

Think more in terms of weeks, because a week is a more finite, manageable time increment. It provides enough flexibility to find a time to meet. But it's not so long that action is put off "until you get around to it."

For example, O'Brien-Gere Engineering was trying to develop a better short- and long-term plan. The firm's management engaged a consultant to help it put together a comprehensive business plan. The purpose of the business plan was to develop a five-year target, and to detail annual plans within the five-year period.

The scope of the five-year and annual targets was very comprehensive:

- It had financial statements, with projected P&L statements for each of the five years
- Goals for growth of the firm for each year, as well as for each branch office, were articulated
- The plan included statements of the markets it wanted to serve, including the business mix between markets, for each of the five years
- The plan even included strategy and the steps by which it would achieve each goal

The firm size at the time was about 300 people. The planning group was made up of 12 to 15 people, the top management of the firm.

They would meet for two days. Three months later they'd come back and meet for two more days. Homework was assigned in between. At the end of the year, they had completed the five-year plan, which included an amazing amount of detail.

They then began implementing elements of the plan.

Thereafter, they met once a year to see how achievement of their plan was progressing—once in the Caribbean to enjoy the fruits of their labor.

This was a little longer-term "temporary." Yet it was a focused effort. Once the plan was implemented, the developmental activity ceased. The group simply conducted annual checkups to see how they were doing on each dimension of their plan and what they wanted to revise.

> When a mission is complete, the results become a part of your firm.
>
> The R&D effort is over.
>
> The temporary task group *dissolves*.

When new issues come along, in six months or a year, other groups can be formed. The process of forming temporary task groups lends itself to increased developmental *action* in your firm.

Sidestreaming

The next condition necessary to cause action involves allowing small temporary groups to work in a way that's uninhibited by the mainstream of activity in your firm.

In Chapter 1, the concept of the cash cow, or production side of the firm, was introduced. The general rule for success in production is smoothness: orchestration, regularity, and care.

If you want to develop something new, however, you often need a small offshoot group—something collateral. Groups of two or three or five employees can accomplish specific results. If you need a larger group because of the size of the new development you envision, more action will result by breaking into subgroups.

Small groups are better able to hide in corners. Two or three people can meet and experiment in off hours in or out of the office. They can accomplish more because they are too small to become bogged down with formalities.

> Experimentation is fostered in environments that lack time pressure, budget and deadline constraints, memos, and all of the other elements essential to your mainstream production activity. Your temporary subgroups need to work in "sidestreams" that are emotionally and even *physically* separate from your firm's mainstream. As new ideas for services or methods or tools are developed, they'll flow into your mainstream for implementation.

McClelland Engineers Inc., a large Houston-based engineering firm, likes to stay on top of its geotechnical science practices. When it develops a new technology, until other firms catch up, it enjoys a clear market edge.

McClelland Engineers Inc. has a small "advanced technology group" that explores new methods in two locations away from the "flow." One is in the basement of their building. The other is inconspicuously hidden among a row of offices.

Some of this group's experiments key to immediate applications on ongoing projects. Other explorations grow independently. When a new method works on a pilot project, the group quickly sells it into other projects. The firm's goal is to diffuse new innovation as quickly as possible. Demonstrations are scheduled. Visiting employees from branch offices stop down in the basement to see what new "goodies" await them.

The group is largely an overhead function that erupts with periodic, but *unpredictable*, payoffs. This kind of sidestream developmental group is difficult to sustain financially when backlog is light. Yet, it is essential to McClelland Engineers Inc.'s long-term success as a leader among geotechnical firms.

> The membership of a small experimenting group can come from different parts of your firm. If the issue is especially critical or requires the commitment of the owners, then one of the principals should be a member.

In the case of McClelland Engineers Inc., at least one person was a part of "management." Others were sophisticated technical professionals.

Junior firm members can participate in some development activities without senior members.

> But one caution: If a couple of staff members in a firm develop something without the support of the principals, and are ready to implement their idea, the principals may react by saying that they're not ready to take the action.

> The rejection builds frustration. Be sure the group has the authority to act on their ideas.

Another concept related to side group experimenting is the *manageableness* of the issue. "Global" issues, such as a complete overhaul of all of your firm's managerial processes, are not suitable for immediate action.

> Remember, the whole purpose of this chapter is to develop a climate for action. Huge programs that may take years are not going to give you much of a feeling of progress.

One way around this dilemma is to break a big issue into bite-size segments. Let a small group develop and solve one bite-size segment in a short amount of time, such as two weeks, four weeks, or six weeks.

For instance, if your goal is to automate your practice, the process can be broken into segments, each with a short timeframe.

Identify the functions that should be automated: four weeks.

Identify which functions can be automated most easily, and set priorities: two weeks.

Gather information about computer systems. Evaluate their potential for your firm's application: six weeks.

Schedule demonstrations of the most promising three or four computer systems: four weeks.

You'll experience measurable and frequent progress toward your goal and enjoy the exhilaration of results.

The satisfaction will lead to the next step, and the next. Even the largest of goals can be achieved in this way.

One other fact about the membership of small developmental groups:

Members of collateral groups need to be volunteers.

Don't assign people to the group. If they don't put their hand up, they have a reason. They may have the interest but no available time. Or they may have no interest.

You'll also find that some part-timer from a nearby college may put up a hand. Your volunteer could be someone you would not normally think of as appropriate. Yet, you'll discover that these volunteers often make unexpectedly useful contributions.

In some situations, firms have discovered summer students who happen to have had extensive experience and expertise with computers. They were able to lead the way into automated drafting for larger firms.

One final expectation related to the action orientation of small sidestream groups:

Don't look for a report.

Keep the amount of paperwork to a minimum. The amount of *action* should be maximum. Groups should be able to come back and say, "Here's what we want to do. Let's do it."

Experimentation

An experimenting firm is one with an action-oriented attitude.

Go ahead and do something.

See what works and what doesn't work.

Repair it, refine it.

And, then go out and try it again!

A *repetitive* process is needed. First, make an initial attempt at something. Evaluate the results of your effort. Then refine your procedure. Make a second attempt. Refine that effort and conduct a third attempt. Nothing happens until the first new idea is tried. If you wait until your idea is sharpened and "ready," action may never occur. Act on your first idea.

Another commitment you should make is to constantly *test everything* in your firm. Excellent firms have a willingness to experiment and to test all aspects of their practice.

You can become comfortable when your firm has been doing well. Because of your comfort, and the success you've enjoyed, you may develop a reticence to continue to experiment. Remember the old engineering adage:

If it's not broken, don't fix it!

However, while it may not be broken, it could always be better. If some aspect of your firm is going well and you change it, then you do, in fact, have something to lose. You have a risk.

Even when something is going well, you can begin testing variations in some small way. Then you have a chance to do some refining.

One of the clients of the BSW Architects firm in Tulsa is a nursing home. One of the observations that one of the principals, Chief Boyd, made was that patients were receiving piecemeal service.

Gaps in service existed that were not being addressed by anyone. Energy consumption and room comfort were not being monitored. Meal service was difficult to plan. Emergency situations were not always easy to detect quickly. Invoicing for individualized services was expensive and cumbersome.

In reading a book on preventive maintenance, Boyd began to see an opportunity for *continuing* services with his nursing home client. The services had a mixture of both architectural and nonarchitectural components. And the services could be handled by some of the computer equipment that already was in place in his firm and was being used in the design of the nursing home.

BSW Architects established and set up a small local telephone company. They designed computer linkages so they could provide full service for the total nursing home with a smaller number of telephone lines than number of beds. (Not all residents would be on the phone at one time, so they reduced phone costs without diminishing service.)

Additional services then began growing.

People needed to be awakened at certain times, either for medication or breakfast or daily programs. Reminder calls were all plugged in, on an individualized basis, to the computer. Each resident in the nursing home could be phoned.

If a resident is phoned and no response is received within a certain amount of time, the nursing station is instantly alerted, automatically. Potential disasters can be averted.

Energy consumption in the entire nursing home is also monitored by the computer. A considerable savings results.

Food service was another area for increased service opportunity. In many nursing homes, residents prefer to fix their own meals. They also have the option of buying meals from the nursing home and eating in the dining room. The resident needs to be able to change his or her mind at the last moment.

The managing of individualized and changing requests presents a problem of both accounting cost and food preparation predictability. Now patients have only to make a telephone reservation.

The computer takes care of reservation for the food, requesting of the type of menu, and billing at the end of the month.

The service uses several of the long distance companies. Each patient's call is always transmitted at the *lowest* long distance costs. The continued service provided by BSW Architects through their little telephone company is more extensive than just a telephone service.

All of these services are provided for the nursing home by BSW Architects on a monthly fee basis. The concept saves the residents money, saves the nursing home money, and produces a continuing monthly income for the professional firm.

As problems are eliminated during initial service tests at the first nursing home, BSW Architects will be able to provide an even better service to the other nursing homes owned by those clients. Eventually, the process will be demonstrated to other nursing homes, which allows BSW Architects to expand the number of facilities being served by the identical system.

And BSW Architects' office, a 12-foot by 12-foot space with one employee, is all that's needed to monitor the computer system and to take care of a large number of facilities that could be included under a continuous maintenance and monitoring service contract.

If any of the services, such as the meal ordering capability, turn out not to be as useful as was originally anticipated, then those services can be modified or eliminated. If new services are needed, they can be added. What's BSW Architects' real risk?

They've simply committed one room and one person for a limited time period.

The *attitude* is what's most important. The principals observed their clients' needs. They responded with some of the capabilities of their firm. And they had a willingness to try it.

O'Brien-Gere Engineering had a long history of water, wastewater, solid waste management, and industrial programs.

A few years ago, the firm's marketing vice president felt that, while the firm's backlog looked good, the towns in upstate New York, which they serviced, might soon develop their own upgraded water and wastewater treatment systems. While a need for service would continue, he perceived that the overall demand that had been supporting the firm could begin to diminish.

The vice president looked for alternatives. He saw that the public demand for the clean up of hazardous waste was growing and that action would soon follow.

The firm began compiling data from interviews with potential clients and used it as additional market research to verify their hunches. Finally, the firm decided to make a significant shift. At that time, roughly five percent of the firm's gross billings came from the private sector; 95 percent was public. They set a goal to reach a 50–50 mix over a four- or five-year period.

The firm began their effort with a marketing blitz in New Jersey, a state which had a significant amount of hazardous waste conditions and, there-fore, clean-up opportunities.

The blitz involved a large number of cold calls by several experienced marketing people. The effort did produce some work. However, from a cost-benefit standpoint, the time and dollars expended to produce that work were high. The blitz approach was therefore discontinued.

A second effort involved national advertising. The firm placed a full-page ad in industrial magazines. The ad talked about the consequences of not cleaning up hazardous waste in an appropriate way. The firm also developed a booklet to help potential clients identify key potential problems. If readers of the ad were interested, they could simply tear out a coupon or telephone for the booklet.

This program precipitated over a thousand inquiries for booklets. And it led to hundreds of thousands of dollars worth of initial fees, including many continuing-service, multiple-phase contracts.

The effort was significant in helping the firm move quickly toward their goal of a 50–50 balance. However, the principals were still not certain that the advertising program was as cost effective as other alternatives may have been.

The point here, though, is that the firm had a *willingness to experiment*.

While they achieved a reasonable amount of success, and the firm grew right through the 1982–1983 recession, many of the people would say that if they had to do it again, they might have tried another way.

> The willingness to act immediately on their idea initially put them in a position to do it better the second time.

Lots of Experiments

Let's say you're beginning to do a lot of tests on a variety of aspects of your firm.

> The more tests you do, the better your chances are for success.
> It's a simple fact that your chances of hitting home runs goes
> up as your number of at-bats go up, regardless of your batting
> average.

The more you test, the more failures you'll have. But you're also going to have more successes. You need to conduct a large number of tests before success, and excellence come your way. First, you begin to look for a variety of possible new markets. In fact, you should brainstorm for a large number of possibilities. Check out several of the best ones more carefully. Then you can narrow your focus to five or six of the most promising. You can eventually organize efforts to win work in each of those markets, so that you begin to see which ones, in fact, pay off.

Ultimately, you can do as much pretesting and data gathering as you wish. But the bottom line is: "We have to try it to find out."

When O'Brien-Gere Engineering began to identify the need for hazardous waste clean-up as a potential market area, they also tested other markets. Hazardous waste clean-up was the one that began to pay off.

McClelland Engineers Inc. is a firm involved in offshore and onshore geo-technical work. The principals began looking at alternative markets after the oil glut hit. By that time, of course, the hazardous waste market had matured, and was not as strong; the government was diverting funds to the Department of Defense.

Yet the firm has been attempting to enter the hazardous waste market by competing with firms that had already come into that market, three or four or five years previously.

> Success comes not just from knowing what the market is and when the best moment exists to enter it. You need a process for *continuously* testing markets or for testing different new pro-cesses or services in your firm. Lots of testing needs to occur before you'll stumble on to the kind of opportunity that returns *significant* rewards.

While the offshore geotechnical firm was late entering the hazardous waste market, it does have a laboratory where experiments are conducted.

They play. And these experiments develop new "gidgets and widgets." Some of the widgets don't really do much. But some do. All that's needed for success is for one experiment to work every now and then for them to maintain a state-of-the-art position in the offshore industry. The only way the testing group is going to achieve these top results is to constantly experi-ment.

Even if only a small percentage of the firm's experiments work, it can expe-rience *considerable* success. The size of their billings expand, as existing clients engage the added services. And the firm can develop a competitive edge as it provides a fuller range of services, many of which are *exclusive* to the firm.

Low-Cost Experiments

In many instances, the cost of conducting an experiment is less than the cost of proposing and planning it. When this happens, you have an opportunity for inexpensive learning. Instead of analyzing and reanalyzing, ask what would it cost to find out by doing it?

A little subgroup, in an alternative way, can always scavenge some material. It can create a way to inexpensively try something: a few phone calls, off-hours contacts, lunchtime meetings, sometimes stealing a couple of hours out of a business day.

The activities may be virtually invisible.

Employees can be doing all of this experimenting *outside* the mainstream of your firm's normal activity.

Corgan Associates is a "corporate" character architectural and interiors firm in Dallas, serving the corporate office market. Suzanne McKee, director of marketing, observed that with all the new office buildings in Dallas, the older office buildings were experiencing a rise in vacancy ratios.

One of the firm's goals was to increase the size of its interiors department. The principals approached the owners of these large old office buildings with proposals to renovate a floor or two at a time.

First, they developed a brochure showing how well historic buildings complement the contemporary ones. The detail, the intricacies, and the warmth and charm of the older buildings was contrasted against the characterists of the newer buildings.

They also invested the time of the marketing director and one of their professional design staff. The two employees made calls on some prospective clients, brochure in hand. Sure enough, they began generating interiors projects.

Later, the two discovered that the firm's designers preferred doing construction over renovation. While the market was hot, and a large number of potential projects could be anticipated, the firm walked away from the opportunity. Yet, the principals could not have envisioned that their staff would not like to do renovation.

The only way to find that out is to do it.

What did the learning cost?

Nothing really. The firm did secure a few projects along with several thousands of dollars in fees. When it found that the work wasn't what the staff wanted to do, it shifted into other markets. The cost of the brochure was quickly recovered.

Some firms do "thorough analyses." Employees read books. They attend workshops. And, when they add up all the costs of learning about markets, and of analyzing potential markets, and of meeting and discussing marketing direction, the cost could be more than making a brochure and conducting a few marketing calls.

One of the associated criteria for success in inexpensive learning is that the tests need to relate to your client. In fact, many of these tests are best performed when you say to your client,

"We want to test a new service. While *we're* going to invest extra time, the experiment, which could reap major dividends for you, won't cost *you* a cent. Would you work with us on it?"

Your client is going to see that he or she has virtually everything to gain and nothing to lose. And you gain client-relevant input all the way through your experimenting process.

The Denver office of Dames & Moore had a special technology group. This group's job was to develop advanced technologies to keep their firm current with the state of the art.

However, the R&D activity done by this group was not done in the office, in isolation. It was actually done in the *field*, at the client's office or project site.

The technology group would identify a project which appeared to have some "frontier qualities," unique aspects that seemed appropriate for state-of-the-art exploration. They would apply additional support to the project, *beyond* what was normally needed. The firm's profit margin on that project would therefore be reduced.

The firm was looking for opportunities. Placing R&D people in the field in an actual project situation to develop the new technology can lead to power-ful long-term success. The client worked with them.

If new developments result, fine. If not, the client is not unhappy, because he or she received a lot of extra effort and attention.

What is the cost? Essentially, it is diminished profits for a given job.

You don't have to use this approach on every project. But you can make a commitment to sacrifice some of your profit margin on a percentage of your jobs in order to do R&D that can give you added capability on many other projects. It's this form of inexpensive client-based learning that can lead you to longer-term excellence.

Environment for Experimentation

An action orientation also requires an *environment* within which the experimenting can occur. While production-oriented environments feature systems and ways to measure achievement, experimenting environments require room for slippage, room for redundancies, room to play, and an environment that rewards exploration and new ideas.

A small architectural firm in Wisconsin, The Hawkweed Group, was design-ing one of its early solar houses. The solar heating storage in this case was a rock bed.

The rocks had been cleaned and washed and were being stored outside. It turned out that the rocks had been outside for a good part of the winter. As construction was completed, they were loaded into their bins in the storage area of the house.

Everything seemed fine. Construction was completed. The owner moved in. And the cold winter came.

Excess solar-heated warm air was being drawn through the rock beds for nighttime heating. But—while warm air should have risen from the rock beds, in the heat cycling system, *cold* air was coming into the house.

The clients called the architect and said,

> "You said that when the sun went down, warmth was going to be stored beneath the floor in these rocks. And, then warm air would begin rising up into our house. All we're feeling are tremendous *cold* drafts coming in!"

The rocks had become cold during the previous winter. And, because of their mass, they had *stored* all that cold, and had never really warmed up.

It was clearly an oversight, although when you're working in a frontier technology, perfection is difficult to achieve. The firm now knows that all rocks to be used for heat storage should be left in the sun and kept warm.

The second year of use in the house was considerably better. The rocks had "recovered." The system was now working perfectly.

In an experimenting context, the client can be told,

> "This is an experiment. We're going to be trying some new things that *could* give you unusual benefits. But, the idea is new. Will you work with us?"

Your client should not be treated as an uneducated patron who wouldn't understand. Share your ideas. An attitude of experimentation will develop.

On each and every project you do, *some* aspect can be experimental. By definition of experiment, the risk of failure is higher.

When two employees try something different, some redundancy often occurs. Let it occur. The experimentation can also lead to something new, and to something quite advantageous to your firm in the long run.

And, if one of these experiments does not work, you have to say,

> "We understood what happened. It was a good attempt. We'll make sure it doesn't happen the second time!"

You have to tolerate mistakes and not expect perfection, especially when you're working in frontier areas.

You have to be able to digress periodically, to play with ideas, to tolerate the inevitable mistakes, and to be willing to spend a few thousand dollars and a few weeks before you can expect results.

If the cost to find out is prohibitive, you should either back off or figure out a way to reduce your costs or your risks. "Prohibitive" is the point at which you would likely damage the regular production side of your firm. The number could be one percent of your gross billings, or four percent or half a percent.

But, you'll find it's often less expensive to just "try it and find out" than to spend as much time and money analyzing your concept to death.

Another aspect of an experimenting context is the concept of the Innovator. This is a person who moves an issue. The Innovator is defined as a person who has an extensive capacity to create new ideas, and an equally extensive capacity to take risks. Innovators will commit "all" on virtually every idea. The Innovator is often the person we look to and say, "Here's our leader!"

Frank Lloyd Wright was one innovative champion among architects. He had his own unique ideas about his profession, and backed these ideas up with action his entire career. Books were written about him. Legends of his deeds became folklore. He established the Taliesin Foundation, which is still in existence.

Frederick Law Olmsted is such a hero among landscape architects, T. Y. Lin among structural engineers.

The Princeton Energy Group had two passive solar specialists, both named Bill. One worked on heating systems, the other on cooling systems. References would be made to "Warm Bill" or "Cool Bill." In fact, the principals of the firm began championing these two as technical giants in their areas.

Both Bills liked to experiment.

"Cool Bill," for example, did some unique field tests with "cool pipes"— earth-to-air heat exchangers. He dug trenches and put in polyethylene pipes with temperature gauges at intervals. He filled the trenches. And then he began to measure the cooling effect at varying trench depths, as air was being drawn through the pipes, at varying speeds.

This kind of testing and experimenting is *essential* in building special proficiency in your firm. When that proficiency develops around a person, you have an innovative leader.

Typically, an innovator is the kind of person who is prepared to "do or die" for the cause. Even if you don't want "it" done on company time, the innovator is so self-directed that he or she is going to do it anyway.

To foster an experimenting context, you need to sponsor that person. Support some of the experimenting activity on company time. And if your firm *doesn't* have all the support needed, say,

> "We will try and pay for the materials. But, we're not having a great year. Could you contribute some of your time on the side? And, when I can, I will even get out in the field and work with you."

The third aspect of an experimenting context is diffusion of the good, proven ideas throughout your firm.

In a one-, three-, or six-person firm, diffusion is not difficult. You sit next to one another. But when you have 20 or 40 people and especially when you have branch offices, diffusion of a concept becomes increasingly difficult. In fact, an innovative leader can be ostracized.

> "Well, that works okay in the Chicago office. But, it won't work in the Minneapolis or Los Angeles offices. That's simply the kinds of jobs they have in Chicago."

Diffusion of innovation is best achieved by *demonstration* of the new idea, especially in a nonthreatening way.

> "Take a look at what George is doing. Let me know what you think of the idea and how it might be refined or applied in other ways."

New experiments, new discoveries, and new applications can be sparked by the first one, if diffusion is done in a way that adds recognition to those you'd like to see adopt the new ideas.

If someone raises his or her eyebrows and shows interest, after you create the exposure, then ideas will eventually spread from one employee to another. Many times you can unintentionally arouse jealousies. Someone says,

> "Hey, we've been doing it this way for five years! And, this is how we're going to do it!"

You have to be sure that what you do does not create a threat for others in your firm. Low-risk exposure, without pressure to adapt, may be the best approach.

One of the principal's jobs is to reduce the threatening climate.

Let the people who want to experiment do so. Maintain an exposure. But, let others "do it the old way" if they wish.

At BSW Architects, the automated firm, new computer buffs, as they come into the firm, seek an area where a new application is needed. They spend hours of their own time writing a new program to perform the new function. They schedule "mini in-house seminars" to spread the ideas.

The goal is to create an eager and open climate for peer sharing.

In McClelland Engineers Inc., the R&D group works with new technologies to keep the firm at the front of their state-of-the-art. Field teams are scattered all over the world in other offices. But every time these field staff visit Houston, they pass through the laboratory to find out what the group has been developing.

Ideas tend to be diffused by regular visits from out-of-town people to the laboratory. The pride taken in the R&D group produces a climate of anticipation of great new ideas and an eagerness to learn them.

One final aspect of an experimenting context is: Set few objectives at any one time in your firm.

> Any more than two objectives is no objective.

Two, in fact, seems to be a magic number. Jim Leu is in charge of marketing for the northeast United States for Camp Dresser McKee, a large Boston-based engineering firm. Paraphrasing Leu,

> "Every year we set our objectives. And, the maximum number is two."

> "We found that whenever we try to set six or eight or twelve objectives, absolutely *nothing* happens."

Leu's group begins working on those two particular goals. The staff sets a time limit of six months or a year. Long time periods are provided to achieve only one or two goals. And, when those are achieved, the group moves on to another pair of goals.

You need to develop a focus on a smaller number of goals. Your chance of achieving them will be greater.

One final comment for the one-, two-, and three-person firms. You may be asking,

> "Well, how do we get subgroups? How do we develop collateral systems, because I *am* the system!"

A *portion of time* in your day might be set aside to do collateral work. If there are two or three in your firm, then maybe set aside two hours a week. And use that time to work on your ideas. Don't let other pressures conflict with that time.

You'll end up with powerful results.

Some firms become proficient in passive solar design. Other firms become proficient in computers. The development pattern seems consistent in the design professions. One person, or two or three people, begin puttering around, and experimenting with some ideas. They do it "in the corner."

But the point is, they *do* it. They take action.

CHAPTER 3

BEING CLOSE TO YOUR CLIENTS

Action orientation is a condition of excellence that takes place within a firm. It may or may not be noticed by the clients who benefit from it.

This chapter focuses on attributes of excellence that clients can hardly help noticing—attributes of client-responsiveness that generate *direct* benefits to both your firm and your clients. There are four segments in the chapter—each one a path to being, or getting, close to your client.

- Use services to expand revenue
- Put quality above all else
- Stress the unique
- Listen to clients

Use Services to Expand Revenue

Services as the key to both extending the amount of revenue your firm produces and to establishing greater excellence in your firm is more than just doing a good design or providing good reports or studies. It includes the excellence of what you do. It also includes the extent of your services, which is linked to your firm's fundamental commitment to giving more service than clients may expect. It has to do with better management and marketing, as well.

Principals in a firm play a critical part in the service orientation. Most principals tend to be consumed by day-to-day routines.

A variety of tasks can fill a day and a principal can work 8 or 10 or 12 or even 15 hours a day, 6 or 7 days a week. But the tasks tend to be shorter-term, immediate-results types of activities.

One key role of a principal is to maintain a longer-term perspective. Even if you have a one-person firm, you may have to adopt a "collateral" approach, taking a few hours each week to set up a *temporary* environment in which you can do some longer-term thinking.

If you have a two- or three-person firm, perhaps what you need to do at the end of the day or on Friday for an hour or two is to get together away from your office where there are no short-term symbols, such as telephone memo slips, to distract you.

One principal who, with a longer-term view, developed tremendous benefits for his firm was Rick Taylor, a biologist with a large environmental firm, Dames & Moore. Taylor was working with a petrochemical company in New Orleans. As part of his work on the project, he established a project office *inside* the petrochemical company's office. He generally spent four out of five days a week in the project office.

What happened?

While Taylor was working on project A, he would have lunch in the employee cafeteria. Over time he met many *new* employees of the client's company. Taylor gradually became part of the relationship network in his client's organization. He was listed in the employee telephone directory. He took his vacations on a rotation with others who were actual employees.

Client employees perceived Taylor as "one of them." He became a bridge; he was seen as part of the petrochemical company, and he was also seen as part of Dames & Moore.

When Taylor was eating in the cafeteria, he'd meet an employee from another division in the company. That person would be talking about a project and some kinds of problems. Taylor would say, "Let's sit down and outline something that would help you solve your problem."

He would develop a proposal for the employee, type out the proper paperwork, have the paperwork authorized. And, he'd give his firm a sole-source contract to do that project.

Taylor's network of contacts, called a "genealogy," began to grow. As he began understanding the kinds of needs different client employees had, Taylor no longer cared about whether it was project A or B or C or D. Each job was part of a longer-term perspective.

Taylor was looking at the broader variety of needs in the client company. And, he simply "took care" of those needs in a total, sole-source way. Taylor's perspective toward the client was, "Rather than saying we were doing a $10,000 project or a $50,000 project, let's just say we're going to do one-and-a-half to two million dollars a year for that client."

> It didn't matter whether it was a few large projects or a lot of little ones.

The Harris Design Group is a small interior architecture firm in Washington, D.C. Many interior designers practice in Washington, D.C. Multitudes of office buildings support a lot of commercial practices. However, one of the longer-term perspectives that Bob Harris, the principal of this firm, has is that while many new jobs come up, few firms service clients on a long-term basis.

One of the biggest problems that many interiors clients have is obtaining quality millwork. It seems like a small detail. Yet it ends up being a major part of the cost of many projects and is one of the "pains," in terms of having on-time, accurate delivery for a client. As a result of these observations, Harris's firm has undertaken two major efforts. Harris and one of his employees established a millwork company. And, second, his firm became increasingly oriented toward long-term computerized facility management. It's a preventive maintenance program applied to interior architecture.

The employees began to work, on a "day-to-day basis," looking for changing uses in client organizations. They'll go into an organization and update just 10 workstations. Then, they may begin developing a larger plan, then update another six stations. And while they're doing the six stations, they may also upgrade the client's lobby.

Harris has been working with some clients on a continuous basis for years. He does not refer to a job with a $100,000 fee or a $50,000 fee, but says, "This client is going to need about $20,000 of work, each and every month."

This orientation is similar to Taylor's for Dames & Moore. Harris has a smaller scale of service and a smaller firm. Harris does his client's initial facilities, and then does all their other facilities. He just keeps updating. He also has a county as a client, including its hospital, its offices, and a variety of other facilities.

All of these contracts are sole-source. They are not out "on the street." They are not low-bid priced proposals.

The trust has been built. The service quality is established. Harris simply is taking care of his client, applying a long-term perspective with long-term rewards.

When a problem arises, it shouldn't have to become a grave situation before the principals personally intervene. A principal can address the problem with project staff members, or without them—depending on the situation. But it is the *principal* that should personally service problems or situations, either by "cutting them off at the pass," or by taking remedial action after the fact.

A principal's intervention is an emphatic service message.

A former president of O'Brien-Gere Engineering, Sam Williams, mentioned once that he was chatting with a client he had helped bring into the firm and with whom he had a good personal relationship. "How are my guys doing for you?"

The client answered, "Well, I'm not sure, frankly, that I am getting exactly what you told me I would be getting."

That's a significant concern to hear in the middle of a project.

Williams went back to his office and read the contract. It seemed consistent with what was supposed to be happening. But then he found that the project team had never actually read the contract. They were doing the job the way they had done similar jobs in the past and had not carefully looked at the specific notes or the contract.

In fact, Williams's project people were not performing in the way they were supposed to. Williams intervened and corrected the situation.

This "hands-off" phenomenon happens more frequently in firms in which the marketing person and the project people are different individuals. Large firms, incidentally, do not have an exclusive claim to this problem. It can occur in a firm of only 12 or 15 people.

The problem usually begins with the principal; typically it is the principal's good relationship with the client that leads to the job. Once the job is in-house, the principal then gives it to a designer or a chief engineer or project manager with instructions to "take care of the project." Now and then, the principal may monitor progress.

Firms that have separate marketing staffs often have the marketing person leave the scene when the job is secured. In too many instances, the marketing person who began the work with the client turns the "contact" over to what is called "professional staff" at the point of development of proposals or presentations.

After the job is done—three months, six months, or a year later—the marketing person gets back in touch with the original client. That scenario has vulnerabilities and liabilities.

> When the principal who made the promises—and developed a personal trust relationship with that client—leaves the scene, the client is left dangling. It's not intentional neglect. But it *feels* like it to the client.

It's clear to the client, especially when dealing with a large firm, that this key principal cannot work full time on the project. However, the marketing person or key principal should always meet with that client, periodically, during the course of a project and ask: "How are my people doing for you?" "Are they doing the job the way you want?" "Are there things that you would like us to do that would make the service even better?"

In a way, the principal is looking over the staff's shoulder. But he or she is giving the client a "third party," a neutral authority to "see how things are going."

Even if your client says, "They're doing just fine," you can say, "I'm delighted to hear that! Are there things we can do to refine our service even further?"

> Because we are human, we are not perfect. We need to monitor a job to be sure things are as good as they can possibly be. It's client quality control. We cannot check our own work. The monitoring must be done by a third party with authority to fix things, a principal.

An excellent firm consistently gives a *visible* message of service commitment. It's not just a verbal one that disappears when the sales pitch is over.

Another signal of excellent firms is that they constantly listen to clients. This listening includes measurement of the results of your projects.

First, from a "professional" standpoint, architects can look at building issues of which clients may not be aware. Engineers can look at aspects of soil erosion, materials cracking, and 101 other things that a client often will not be sensitive to.

Second, you also must measure performance in areas that clients are aware of. That's called "feedback." It involves constantly listening to and monitoring your clients.

It is easy for professionals to say, "We listen to our clients!"

Probably 99 percent of the design firms would say that. Yet in many cases, professionals think they are listening to their clients when they are not. Real excellence is attained through a *consciously structured system* for ensuring measurement of performance through feedback.

The first example was cited once before, in Chapter 1. In 1982, the AIA held a small meeting of select clients to identify client concerns related to energy. The AIA was seeking to develop energy conservation programs that would respond to client needs.

These were not small clients. They were major directors of facilities. One was from the Westinghouse Corporation. One was from the Department of Defense. One represented an entire university system with several campuses. These clients awarded a large number of projects, new construction and restoration, of a variety of sizes, on a regular basis.

The discussion was not limited to energy. At one point, the clients began talking about what they liked and disliked about the architects and engineers who served them. When they discussed problems, they all agreed on the two biggest:

> The first big problem is known as "bait and switch."

At a presentation or in a written proposal, the engineer or the architect or the interior designer says, "I, as principal, will be with you. I'm behind your project and will be working on it personally."

And, after the client hires the firm, that's the last they ever see of that principal. (This is truer of larger firms than it is with a one- or two-person firm in which the principal is the firm.) But, even in dealing with firms of 7 or firms of 12—which may include over 80 percent of all firms—clients are consistently sensitive to and searching for someone who is being straight with them. The basic assumption of these clients was that virtually all the principals they dealt with were not being straightforward with them.

> The second major problem that all the meeting participants
> had was that when either architects or engineers or designers
> finish a project, it's the last they ever see of them.

In not returning to a project afterwards, firms are not demonstrating care to see how our clients are feeling after they begin using the project. In fact, the clients at the meeting seemed to have a sense that most firms are noncaring.

Here are a couple of examples of how these problems have been addressed by some firms, through systematic feedback. The first is known as an "external audit."

Graham Associates, a Dallas-Fort Worth firm of roughly 100 consulting civil engineers, decided to do an external audit. An outside public relations consultant and a business manager in their firm, both of whom did *not* work on projects specifically, formed a two-person team.

The two began paying visits to clients. Some were past clients. Some were ongoing clients. The purpose of the visits was to listen and to get performance feedback.

They were told by one client, "Just as I got comfortable with your first project manager, you moved him off the project and brought me a second one. And, when we finally started to get comfortable with the second one—who I really didn't like as well as the first—then all of the sudden along came the third one. And, we had to reeducate him to our style." The client felt jerked around.

This is an example of project manager-level bait and switch. The firm just wasn't conscious of it. What simply happened is that a new marketing situation came along that demanded the expertise of a specific project manager, he was moved off job A because he was the most appropriate one for job B.

Firms don't do this kind of thing to annoy existing clients. The second and third project managers were technically competent. Firms simply don't perceive that the reassignment is such an irritant to clients.

Once Graham Associates' office discovered the problem, they changed their management structure to ensure that the original project manager was on the project all the way through.

Similar feedback was received by a partner of Dames & Moore in its Seattle office. One of the firm's clients, someone who had worked with the firm for many years, had slowly been giving the firm a diminishing amount of work. The partner called on the client to discover why this was happening. Dames & Moore has a "key person contact program," which is, in fact, a structured feedback system.

The partner, in this case, happened to have been the person who brought the client to the firm originally. He had a long-time friendship that went back over 20 years. The client said, "Joe, every time I meet with your firm I'm dealing with new faces. Some are good. Some are not as good. But I just don't know *who* I am dealing with on a consistent basis. Now, if you want to tell me that *you* are back on the scene and that you will manage and overview all my projects, I have a lot of work that I can give you!"

In this case, the partner simply looked at his client and said, "I'm your man!"

And there they were. While marketing resulted, success was actually achieved through feedback. Most firms tend to look at projects in a technical way, asking, "Who is the most appropriate person, technically?"

Often we may not think as carefully about maintaining the quality of the relationship. Both the Dames & Moore client and the Graham Associates clients were saying, "It's important to us to be able to maintain a long-term, consistent relationship with *one* person in your firm."

> It's the kind of caring that clients need. And, it's essential to a regular feedback system. Excellent firms *all* have carefully structured feedback systems.

The principals of firms—the chief executive officers of larger firms, the partners at the top, the people who make management decisions—should also spend time out in the field. This includes client project meetings, marketing calls, project site visits, open houses, and all other environments in which clients are involved.

The majority of firms being small, most principals do maintain contact with clients. Often—and this is probably truer for larger firms—the heads of the firm, the principals, become increasingly involved with financial management, marketing strategies, and long-range planning. In many cases—because they have delegated well—they begin to lose touch with *individual* clients.

The reason that principals need to be "in the field," as most broadly defined, is that principals must do a lot of listening to clients and a lot of observing of client environments.

> The best way of achieving this goal is in an "elbow-rubbing" way, on a frequent basis. That way, the principal can notice *patterns*, see *shifts* in the marketplace, and develop an *intuitive sense of client expectations*.

The benefits are, first, that principals can then direct the firm in a way that maximizes its responsiveness to clients and, in a larger sense, to the marketplace.

The second benefit is that the empathy is also built *internally*. Principals begin to understand why project architects, project engineers, designers, and technicians do things the way they do.

Instead of being blinded by the narrow scope of work on projects and dealing only with day-to-day issues, you should periodically sit in on meetings with clients when they are not looking at a project. This will help you think about the fuller picture of needs, concerns, and perceptions of your client and of your larger marketplace.

> A broader view improves the quality of the first-hand experience that you develop.

Service is an area where overspending is appropriate, even productive. When design professionals meet with clients who have selected their firm to negotiate a fee and the client says, "Well, if you can't do the job for three-and-a-half percent," which might be a percent-and-a half less than what the firm needs, "we can sure get it done for that down the street."

The fact is, the aspects of your firm or your service that are "me too" *can* be purchased down the street for a little less.

Not only in negotiating your fees, but in distinguishing your firm, you need to begin by asking yourself, "What is it that really separates us from others?"

That "something" needs to be tangible, specific, and useful.
From a client's perspective, most firms are basically the same.

One easy way to understand the importance of this perception is to turn the tables. Think about hiring other professionals, such as accountants. You might, in your community, identify three to five accounting firms. Without much question, they could *all* service your firm's needs.

What separates Number One from Number Two?

You can assess accountants' technical skills only up to a certain level. They all seem to know what they are doing. They all understand the IRS. They all understand the forms that have to be filled out. They all provide you with guidelines on financial planning.

Some are friendlier than others. So, distinguishing decisions are often based on personal relationship; "I feel more comfortable with George than I do with Don. Therefore, I'm going to hire George."

Or, "George's office is in my building. I can get to him a little more easily. I'll hire him over Don for that reason."

But, if you look at two accounting firms, or five accounting firms, what are the unique qualities that distinguish one from another? And, that is the point you need to think about here.

In what ways can you overspend on service, quality and reliability to set yourself apart?

You can provide:

- Faster service
- Long-term service
- Informational service
- Broader service

For example, Chief Boyd, a principal in BSW Architects in Tulsa, described earlier, has a saying:

"We have to provide a little *more* than everybody else."

A developer client was putting up an office building. He had a funding commitment from a bank. But as they were nearing completion of design and getting ready to move ahead with the construction, the bank folded. His developer was hanging on the line, with his permanent financing gone out the window.

Boyd began exercising his contacts with other lenders. He found a way in which his client could use another land parcel that was not being developed at the time, to leverage an even stronger loan position with another financing institution.

He also quickly conducted additional feasibility studies for his client. The studies showed that his client could also increase profitability if he increased the building by an additional story.

They actually expanded the building. With his CADD systems, Boyd was able to expand the size of the building—in terms of redesign and new construction documents—within roughly 48 hours.

His client ended up with a better project, with better financing, with a more profitable situation, without any compromise in the architecture, and without any delay in his original timetable.

That's the kind of quality that Boyd sees as "getting more without paying any more." Speed, in this case, was a critical part of the added service.

Arthur Gensler Associates, one of the largest architectural firms and also the largest interiors firm in the United States, has more than full CADD capability. The firm also began developing software for *continuing* services.

Record drawings are stored in their computer files. The firm then developed a preventive maintenance program that can be applied to each project. Being in a position to instantly produce current building data, and to monitor and assess all aspects of the facility, the firm does continuing design—and redesign—and redesign. This process has become known as computerized facility management.

Arthur Gensler Associates' clients receive a special continuing service—because of the CADD system and the firm's management process—that cannot be received from other firms.

At some point, of course, many more firms will have integrated CADD systems. And, at an even later point, many firms will have continuing facilities management programs. But, until that time, the Gensler firm will enjoy an advantage in offering a long-term service that cannot readily be bought down the street.

Several firms provide newsletters and information update services to their clients. Some are only self-aggrandizing, and tell their clients about their recent "wonderful jobs." However, many provide clients with *usable* information.

Yearwood and Johnson in Nashville, Tennessee, is roughly a 100-person firm. It has an excellent newsletter, *In Progress*, that discusses different projects that the firm has done—with helpful concepts as to how and why a particular idea solved a specific problem. However, in order to service their hospital clients more effectively, they also have a special monthly bulletin called *Code Perspective*.

One of the biggest problems facing hospital administrators is keeping up with constant code changes that affect hospitals. The firm provides its clients with a single sheet of paper with all relevant code updates. The page may be only half full or two-thirds full—depending on the number of changes that month. But the data provides a unique and useful service.

Hospital administrators who could employ several different architects at any given time, enjoy a service that adds that extra measure.

Some firms conduct seminars on a regular basis for their clients. Many accountants do this with tax law updates. This approach is generally more useful if your firm is serving a geography in which a majority of your clients can attend with only 30 to 45 minutes driving time.

Syska and Hennessey, a national, multiple-office electrical-mechanical engineering firm with its main office based in New York City, was at one time conducting seminars almost monthly, rotating them among their different offices. The firm would highlight key projects, such as Century City in Los Angeles, and conduct a seminar showing key new ideas that had been developed in the course of the project—from which *all* of their clients could learn. In addition, the firm made transcriptions of the seminars available to clients in other cities who could not attend.

The idea provides an added service that costs their clients no more. It's a service that helps set the firm apart.

Cini-Little International, a food-service consulting firm, works with owners, architects and engineers on institutional buildings, industrial buildings, hospitals, hotels, restaurants, and other projects that include food service.

Many architects don't know that the food-service consulting profession exists. They either design that segment of the project themselves or expect that the kitchen equipment suppliers will take care of all the kitchen planning and layout.

The Cleveland office of Cini-Little International, which is a firm of about 100 employees with one-third of them in the Washington, D.C. area, is headed by Ron Kooser. As he developed kitchen layouts, Kooser found that he also had to help clients with diet and menu selection. Then he had to help them with the graphics of their menus. That led to suggestions about the graphics of the environment.

Kooser also found that many people didn't know how to *staff* a facility, so the firm helped them with employment, staffing, and training. The firm also gets into *finances*. Clients seek help in setting budgets, doing feasibility studies, and performing market research analyses.

Cini-Little International does front-end work, such as employee satisfaction, and follow-up work, such as surveys because the industry wants to know how its employees are enjoying the food services.

They've even done menu updating and menu modification and eventually had to help set up tests on pricing—both for commercial restaurants and in-house dining facilities, such as government employee's cafeterias or large corporate cafeterias.

In being sensitive to the marketplace, Kooser began to find that Cini-Little International could not just come in and "design a kitchen." It had to be able to start from the feasibility of putting the entire facility together.

It's an excellent example of sensitivity to the marketplace.

The firm began adding additional services, many of them very subtle. And many of them are not all that expensive: a $1,000 fee for one aspect, a few hundred dollars for something else.

> The principals of Cini-Little International became sensitive to a need for one-stop shopping in a complete array of activities in which people really have very little knowledge. And it became one of the features that sets the firm "a cut above."

Return to the original notion of overspending on service, quality, and reliability:

- With added service, you are talking about added content
- You are talking about follow-through
- You're talking about having all your record drawings continuously available on a computer and being able to provide add-on services
- You're talking about newsletters and updates
- You're talking about preventive-maintenance checks
- You're talking about providing more and more one-stop shopping, including minor services that provide a comfort, and allow your client to stay with one professional, throughout the project

The title of this first section, "Using Services to Expand Revenue," becomes increasingly clear. Not only are you increasing your professionalism, but by listening to the marketplace and by looking for additional opportunities—additional needs to be filled—you are at the same time increasing your revenues. That's a natural way to improve the scope and the profitability of what you do.

When you overspend on service, clients cannot get it down the street.

Put Quality Above All Else

All excellent firms share one trait: an obsession with quality.

> Quality, in fact, is almost synonymous with excellence in the eyes of most design professionals.

An article was written a few years ago in one of the newsletters that serves the design professions. It discussed a "point of diminishing returns." The message in the article was this:

> After 80 or 85 percent of the project budget has been spent, 90 percent of the work may have been completed. For every two additional hours invested, about half an hour's worth of benefits to the project might be received.

> That's the point at which you want to cut off the extra design work, optimizing work-for-gain.

The concept is true from a perspective of immediate project profitability. But it's not as true from a perspective of quality. Professionals who have a quality obsession would hold that:

> It's the last 10 percent that makes the difference between a good job and a great job.

Firms that consistently demonstrate excellence will go that extra ten percent.

In a firm referred to previously, O'Brien-Gere Engineering, one senior engineer who has been with the firm for some time is not known as a great manager. Yet, he was moved into a higher position in the firm because of his high esteem and his extreme technical skill.

In fact, the O'Brien-Gere engineer was made a senior vice president in the firm and given appropriate pay for that position. However, he was asked to function in a senior technical role. People in the firm want their projects to go across his desk before they go to their clients. He is known as a superb quality-control person.

That's an example of "one extra quality step." A highly paid, highly esteemed member of a firm is strictly in charge of quality control, because of his incredible technical proficiency.

Some firms have exceptionally experienced construction field crews. One of the last bastions of job checking, to make sure that everything is right, is to have a good field staff.

Some firms believe construction observation is a place to bring up younger people. Others say it's where the most experienced hands are needed. The firms use employees who have been in the field for many years and have an in-depth skill at spotting flaws—at spotting potential problems and warding them off—and they feature that experience as a quality of service to their clients.

A second example related to quality obsession comes from the professional society for geotechnical engineers. One requirement for membership in their society is that all member geotechnical firms be audited every five years.

An audit is conducted by a team of three other geotechnical engineers. They are generally principals of their firm, people with a depth of experience and not direct competitors.

The team visits a firm for one or two or three days for an in-depth, top-to-bottom examination.

Anything and *everything* is reviewed. And a thorough report is delivered to the firm. Private information, such as the firm's finances, may also be reviewed, but is not normally made public to the society.

The audit is a quality measure.

It's a rare move on the part of a professional society. And, it's perceived as an excellent move at being able to maintain a consistent level of quality in the profession.

Geotechnical engineers who don't want to be audited simply are not members of that society. It's one of the assurances the society provides to show that their members maintain not just a licensing level of competence, but an increasing level of *excellence* consistent with the developing state-of-the-art in the profession.

Generally, design professionals are not known as a haphazard group of people. Most presentations to clients focus on delivering jobs on time, delivering them within budget, and maintaining a level of responsiveness.

Much of this is maintained because of the smallness of most firms. Communications flow reasonably well, enabling firms to keep fairly tight controls on what does happen with the project.

However, quality obsession is that *last* inch, that extra mile, those few extra steps that make the difference between a good job and a great job.

> A quality obsession also includes consistency. It involves a consistent commitment to go for the greatness, and to do what it takes to go from being good to being *excellent*.

Stress the Unique

Return to the negotiating problem discussed earlier: "Well, if you can't do it for 3 percent, I can sure get it for that down the street from a lot of other people."

For every firm, the question about what percentage of business is "me too" and what percentage is truly *unique*—for which it is virtually the *only* firm that can provide that type of help—is a key issue.

Having unique services gives you an excellent market position. First, in negotiating fees, when your client *can't* "get it down the street" you are in a much better position to be fairly compensated.

Second, you're in a good position to establish and maintain an excellent identity. Most firms seem to think that they are capable of doing virtually anything.

An architect will say,

> "Well, we've done hospitals and institutional buildings. There is no reason why we can't do university buildings and laboratories, because those are institutional also.
>
> "They're large scale structures.
>
> "And, we should also be able to do housing and field houses without any problem."

From a client's perspective, however, the same conclusion doesn't hold true.

> Think about the physician who says, "Well, we conduct a general practice. Of course, any given problem that we find in your body is going to be part of that general specialty. And, we treat those things in a routine way. While we haven't actually done triple bypass surgery before, there's nothing really that unusual involved."

Even with specialized heart surgery, a certain percentage of what specialists do is probably "me too" work: checking pulses, taking temperatures, and attending to patients.

The "me too" portion could be 60 or 70 percent, even in this case. But, it's the *unique differences* that set heart surgeons apart from other generalists or specialists.

Many design firms don't try to identify a specialty. We must ask:

- Who *are* we?
- What are we *uniquely* better at than anyone else?
- What is our *difference*?

Even if that difference is only a 10 percent or a 20 percent domain of your practice, you need to identify it. It's an area many firms tend to *avoid* defining, in order to not be limiting. You cannot be all things to all people.

> In terms of professional excellence, identifying your uniqueness allows you to develop a *focus*. And you need not be so narrow in your scope that you become overspecialized, to the point of risk, if the demand for your particular niche diminishes.

You can have two or three areas of concentration and "uniqueness," and you'll still have a unique "groove" that will set your firm apart from others.

Yours should also be a groove in which you have a personal enthusiasm. Make it the kind of uniqueness you *want* to have.

For example, in passive solar design, Rodney Wright and The Hawkweed Group have a unique position in designing all their buildings: they are 100 percent passive solar and, to the extent possible, use only renewable resources.

Wright occasionally suffers from not winning a larger school commission because his clients perceive that he only does smaller-scale, residential "stick construction" projects. While he perceives that there is no reason why he can't do a large school—or a mid-rise office building—and do them in the same passive solar vein, Wright's clients don't always see it that way.

A niche may exclude clients who don't share your direction.

However, Wright does have a unique niche. It's one he enjoys. It's consistent with his personal and professional values. And that commitment is shared by all members of the firm. For all clients who share that interest, he'll find marketing success.

The Hawkweed Group does do programming and drafting and construction supervision. And they do quality design—as many other firms do. But that's part of the "me too" business.

What sets The Hawkweed Group aside is their commitment to passive solar design and the use of renewable resources.

In building systems, Buckminster Fuller stood out with his early dimaxian houses, prefabricated designs, and geodesic domes.

Ezra Ehrenkrantz developed unique skills with the SCSD Stanford project on prefabricated school design, and with his continuing commitment to systems design. Ehrenkrantz thinks in systems terms, in terms of how materials and systems fit together and join. He approaches projects in terms of a marriage of technology with good quality design, and has developed unique sophistication in that area.

SWA Architects, Inc. is a 15-to 20-person architectural firm in Richmond, Virginia, that has unique capabilities in historic renovation.

The two partners, for example, became interested in self-development. They would buy old and under-utilized historic buildings—which are often available at reasonable rates. They became proficient in understanding investment tax credits. And they became developers, feeding the design part of the projects to SWA Architects, Inc.

All employees in that firm have enthusiasm for opening up walls of old buildings, finding old relics, being sensitive to the details of the old buildings, and bringing old buildings back to a charm that's unique to certain historic structures.

That doesn't mean that the firm cannot design new structures. And it also doesn't mean that they don't do contemporary interiors, for instance, in which to accommodate computers and control climate. But these are areas also strongly covered by most other firms.

Their uniqueness lies in their focus on historic preservation, historic renovation, and adaptive reuse of historic facilities. They developed their ability to carry a project from start to finish: developing the project; designing the project; restoring it; finding tenants; and leasing it.

From top to bottom, SWA Architects, Inc. provides full service totally focused on historic renovation in the historic parts of Virginia.

One of the members of the firm has fine skill in watercolor painting and rendering. Every year he creates a "poster" that portrays a historic scene, such as a collage of Richmond. It's a beautiful image, and it's totally consistent with the firm's historic interests. Each watercolor reflects the kind of "tastey old qualities" of the historic nature of that city. The watercolors are reproduced by the firm on an extremely high-grade paper in limited editions. Each copy is signed by the artist.

For instance, out of an edition of 500, they might distribute 200 to 250 to clients. The mayor of Richmond has a framed copy behind his desk. The governor of the state of Virginia also has one behind his desk. The remaining 100 to 150 are donated to the local art museum for sale, with proceeds going to the museum.

One final example of uniqueness comes from Arctic Engineers, an 18-person engineering firm in Anchorage, Alaska, headed by Sid Clarke.

Clarke's background is in R&D. His entire professional interest lies in the development of new systems and new processes. Innovation is what excites him. Consequently, others join his firm because they are also motivated by the same desire for innovation.

For example, Clarke arranged special new technology licenses with some German firms to apply a unique wastewater batch digester system that outperforms others in North America. Clarke is also constantly visiting specialists and researchers at different universities in the "Lower 48."

The firm is constantly involved in the new technologies related to water, wastewater, and solid-waste management. The climate in Alaska also sparks the challenge that demands that type of orientation. Many of their cold weather developments will lead them into work elsewhere because they have unique capabilities.

Arctic's uniqueness lies in its ability to take absolute state-of-the-art, "frontier" technologies—methods that have barely been developed—and work out ways to apply them. Once it becomes a "widely accepted" state-of-the-art procedure, and is adopted by a variety of *other* firms, it moves on to something else.

The firm even manages itself in an R&D fashion. Its office looks like a lot of individuals running around, or clustered in corners, doing a variety of things. It doesn't have the look of a close-knit, well-oiled machine like a football team. Tight management information systems, to control the flow, *don't* exist. The staff is more like a bunch of broken field runners or a variety of loners that are puttering and experimenting. And out of that milieu, they regularly emerge with new technologies and new applications.

It's how they see themselves. And it's how their clients see them in the marketplace.

> The problem of establishing uniqueness is that most firms seem
> afraid of being trapped into a narrow cubbyhole. Yet, from the
> clients' perspective—and this chapter is about getting close to
> the client—they seek firms that have a distinct identity that
> matches the kind of help they are seeking. You do the same
> thing when you seek help from other professionals.

Your uniqueness can relate to geographic identity, such as being the town architect or designer. It could relate to a project specialty, such as historic renovation or wastewater treatment. It could relate to an approach to design, such as passive solar or systems design. It could relate to how you do projects, such as special uses of CADD.

You need to create a doable niche or unique quality. In marketing your uniqueness, you need to present your firm in a way that is totally consistent with the unique identity you *wish* to create. Your promotion, your marketing, your client contacts, the organizations you join, and your technical specialties must be consistent in their focus.

Listen to Clients

Most innovation, in terms of new services, grows from contact with your clients. It comes from the marketplace in the form of suggestions offered by your clients.

Many corporations have a toll-free, customer service telephone line. As people call and complain or make requests, those complaints or requests can also be converted into ideas for possible new services, products, or new opportunities.

(A problem is the flip-side of an opportunity.)

Returning to an earlier discussion about BSW Architects and the extended services they provide to nursing homes, those opportunities came from the principal listening to his client talk about operational problems. Chief Boyd began to see that needs existed for streamlining and extending patient services.

Many firms come up with what they consider brilliant ideas. But they have a hard time selling them to any of their clients.

Because you observe that the marketplace needs something—or that you think it will be useful—does not mean that your client is going to think it's useful. If an idea does not receive acceptance from a client, it's a loser.

Let it go.

> One of the problems design professionals have is that we
> become caught up in practicing our art. The problem, of
> course, is that our art is really an *applied* art. It must have a
> user connection.

You may have an idea that you think is extremely exciting, even though you may be receiving poor responses from your clients. That's when you'll hear, "We need to educate our clients. Our clients don't understand us."

One certain way to evaluate a new idea is to see if you can find an interested user who would be willing to test it.

During their work with food-processing plants, Dave Rigby's Clean Water Engineering firm in Fincastle, Virginia, began to observe that every time *anything* happened, his plant manager client quickly called him up and asked for staff help.

Rigby began to discover, on a monthly basis, that the staff was spending a significant number of hours on a miscellaneous variety of projects. They were generally maintenance types of activities that could come under the heading of handholding. None were major contracts.

Rigby had only been charging fees on a project basis. He felt he'd be "nickel and diming" them if he charged for every 10-minute phone call or half-hour visit.

It was one of his clients who came to Rigby with a proposal, "We would be willing to pay a monthly retainer. The retainer would cover answering phone questions and coming over for odd jobs. Make an estimate of the number of hours you spend," the client said, "and what that should cost. Average whatever you've done over the past few months. Let's work out a reasonable retainer so you can be paid for that time. I know that you have to make a living."

> Most clients who are in business for themselves understand that
> they can't and shouldn't try to get something for nothing. You
> want professionals who serve you to earn a good living—so
> they'll be around to help you next year, too.

The concept began to spread.

One client after another accepted the offer. Rigby now has a number of clients engaged on monthly retainers. The program does beautiful things for the firm's cash flow, profitability, and assurance of repeat work. And the idea came from clients.

Most of Dames & Moore's R&D activity was not done in an isolated laboratory. It was done in the field, among clients, in the client's environment.

When this high-technology firm identified potential new service development opportunities, it would work with the client. It would bring its R&D group *to the client* and work collaboratively to develop the new products.

Probably the one practice that is not widely used by any of the design professions—whether a small or large firm, an architectural, engineering, or interiors firm—is an active program for listening to users.

One of the biggest problems in the design professions is our orientation to present qualifications. It's a conditioned behavior. If you had good answers in school, you received an A. When you went to work in a firm and came up with good project solutions, you received praise and bonuses.

The entire reward system has been geared to good *answers*, rarely to good questions. Most professionals, therefore, intend to engage their mouths more quickly than their ears.

One of the most powerful tools that has been introduced in marketing professional services is the earlier-mentioned process known as the Mandeville Techniques. Developed by Richard E. Byrd, Ph.D., the process is a sophisticated approach to trust-building and relationship-building. It is based on listening, and it's a diagnostic approach.

The Mandeville Techniques process has been learned by over 14,000 design professionals. Success has been dramatic, because it commands such a significant change. Many firms use it as a prerequisite to pursuing a particular project. Yet, it isn't really a "slick sales tool." Its diagnostic approach is helpful all the way through the project.

Once you have a job, your listening skills shouldn't cease. It's a way to be sure your client is happy with what you are doing. Your listening should continue even when the project is done, to see that your client is, in fact, satisfied with the outcome. And, the process should continue afterwards, to see what new needs arise.

Many of the marketing courses advocate continuing service programs and follow-up, all the skills of which center around good listening.

A host of specific techniques go with the Mandeville Techniques process. One design which professionals seem to have difficulty with is the orientation—or in identifying the most important type of data. The key things to listen for are not the physical data, such as how many million gallons a day are required for a treatment plant, or what colors.

> Design professionals, coming basically from the physical sciences, tend to be oriented more toward facts. You need to listen more for *concerns*—for feelings—and for problems.

If a situation exists in which your client does not feel the problem, then no problem exists. Your client will not commit funds, time, energy, or anything else to solving it. Very often, the definition of a problem relies on your observation as a professional. But unless a problem is felt by your client, it isn't a problem, at least it isn't for your client.

In talking about listening to the marketplace, and that "new ideas require an interested user," you'll find that if your ideas are not in synchrony with your client's—if your client doesn't feel the problem and doesn't find your ideas to be responsive to what he or she perceives the problem to be—your proposal for action will not be accepted.

Few firms have developed an "external audit" program, in which people from your firm who are not delivering services on a project go into the field to interview clients. If a project manager is working daily with your client, another principal from your firm—someone neutral—should do the interviewing.

The interviewer is in a neutral position to show interest in your client, to find out "how things are going," and to be exploring to see what other kinds of needs your client has.

This type of program allows your firm to *systematically* identify opportunities by perceiving unfulfilled needs in the marketplace. Then you can begin to develop appropriate responses to those needs.

This chapter has been focused on ways of getting close and staying close to your client. Many firms operate on a regular basis without maintaining broad client sensitivity. That doesn't mean they are not being responsive to their clients. However, they often don't look for opportunities above and beyond the project.

> The concept of looking for and responding to unfulfilled needs has a way of building *revenue* in your firm. It's a way of "expanding the pie."

> The notion of looking for problems that need to be fulfilled and having that quality obsession to go an *extra* step to deliver beyond what others do expands the quality of your services.

> The notion of "uniqueness"—of finding and identifying things you do that nobody else does—begins to set you *apart*.

> A systematic program of listening to your clients—and developing innovations in response to what you hear from your clients—help ensure marketplace acceptance of new innovations.

Those four aspects, applied consistently, will help you achieve and maintain a closeness to your clients and increase your responsiveness in the marketplace. Excellent firms know this.

CHAPTER 4

BUILDING ENTREPRENEURIAL SPIRIT

For a design firm to grow in excellence, unique new services and capabilities must be developed. Chapter 3 makes that clear. *Experimentation* is essential to such development.

> This chapter deals with *autonomy*, or freedom to experiment and try new ideas, and with *entrepreneurship*, or goal-directed development of new technologies, products, services, and capabilities that will give your firm a unique position in the marketplace.

Entrepreneurship also implies a certain spirit. This is not the spirit of products being developed in isolation, as an artist might do on his or her own. It's one that grows with whatever item or service or product being developed for a particular purpose, mission, or specific marketplace. In short, *entrepreneurship is goal-directed*.

> Autonomy, or the freedom to experiment, is nurtured best with "collateral environments," usually a parallel environment that is not subject to pressure from project production or normal management control systems and where fear or failure is not part of the pressure.

Experimental and entrepreneurial activities in firms may be collateral off-shoots of regular projects. They are a form of an R&D effort and may begin independently *or* in response to the pressure of a single project.

Splinter Groups

Entrepreneurial projects work well when undertaken in small groups of people, splinter groups. Typically, splinter groups have from two to eight people. Their work is generally performed in quiet corners or even in separate, more remote, rooms, floors, or buildings, where the people are protected from distractions and pressures that production side staff feel.

McClelland Engineers, Inc., in Houston, houses one part of its material-testing group in the basement and another part on an office floor amid a row of offices. When other staff want to see what's happening, they have to make an effort to *find* the R&D groups. There are no signs.

The Princeton Energy Group, in Princeton, New Jersey, was organized within a typical office corridor arrangement. Two highly creative employees, called "Warm Bill" and "Cool Bill," shared an office that was at the remote end of the suite, where they could have quiet. Their office was a jumble of computers and printouts; nobody went there without a specific purpose.

Led by Harrison Fraker, one of the firm's principals, or by either "Warm Bill" or "Cool Bill," the firm did a number of experimental solar energy studies—many of them carried out independently and separately from the firm's regular projects.

One study experimented with the use of models for measuring daylight, and for testing impacts of different daylighting designs as part of an office building commission. They were trying to maximize the amount of natural lighting and minimize the amount of overhead lighting.

They developed approaches that sharply reduced both initial and continuing costs for their clients. In fact, normal overhead lighting was eliminated from the office building they designed, and still met all lighting standards.

In a second set of tests, "Cool Bill" placed thermocouples along a tube, which was then buried, to measure the change of air temperature. The air was drawn at varying speeds through a tube that was buried at different depths. Those tests provided reliable information for predicting the cooling capacity of earth-to-air heat exchangers, often known as "cool pipes."

While such experiments rarely can be billed as part of a job, the results gave the firm a technical edge. It can lead to the ability to offer services that other firms lack.

Decentralized Structure

The more activities are centralized, the more *controlled* they are. Control aids production.

> One of the conditions that firms require to have excellence is a certain amount of *looseness*. Some events should be allowed to happen spontaneously.

For instance, activities can even have built-in redundancies. Two employees may each do a cost estimate; one might develop a new method for doing it. By being decentralized, people and events are less controllable. And yet, by allowing playful events to occur in the figurative corners of your office, you also increase the chance of unusual and productive new developments.

There will be some lack of coordination. Internal competition may exist. There may even be a certain amount of chaos. And yet, all of this tends to build excitement and *entrepreneurial spirit*.

Dames & Moore has scores of partners with the title "principal-in-charge" (PIC), in 40 or 50 offices around the world—half of them in the United States. One of the management expectations in the firm is that each PIC is expected to develop and conduct an independent practice. Each is expected to identify prospective clients, conduct marketing activities, and serve those clients as part of the firm's practice.

Each PIC is also expected to produce work that will support a certain amount of technical and professional staff, and will maintain standards set by the firm.

In many ways the firm is 100 concurrent and simultaneous practices. However, partners have a real opportunity to conduct very individualized practices under the umbrella of the sponsoring firm.

Duplication of effort can happen. But because of the extreme decentralization, each partner must maintain a practice. The policy sparks entrepreneurship.

One partner has a practice that may support five or six people. Another supports thirty people. A certain amount of peer pressure pushes each partner to upgrade his or her practice.

An excellent example of decentralization among architectural firms is Skidmore, Owings and Merrill (SOM). Suites and offices share the name. But in many ways, that's about all they share. The offices are allowed to compete against one another for a project as if they were two separate firms.

Years ago, the Chicago office developed unique state-of-the-art computer programs. The software was the property of the Chicago office, and the programs they had gave them a competitive edge over other architectural firms, including other SOM offices.

> Internal competition is a powerful and controversial phenomenon in design firms. In many firms, it breeds internal destructiveness.

One of the best examples of destructive internal competition occurred in a large, multiple-office firm. A professional in its Pacific Northwest office developed, over time, extensive relationships with clients in the public utility industry. That person was transferred to an East Coast office of the firm. He was told that his "contacts" would be maintained by others in his former office, and to develop new contacts.

The firm had also initiated a program of individual bonuses. People perceived that personal bonuses were going to be paid for leads and jobs brought into the firm.

The perception by members of the firm was that the system was competitive. They stopped sharing contacts. People in the Pacific Northwest office pursued a project as a "cold-call," without the benefit of existing relationships, and with remote odds of success. The advantage that the transferred professional had built through a close personal relationship with the client was wasted.

While some individual cases of internal competition have been destructive, the dynamic can breed a certain amount of entrepreneurship. And you can avoid loss by shifting from a zero-sum balance ("If I win, then you lose") to a non-zero-sum, or win-win, structure, in which all participants can gain.

The Colorado Springs firm, Rocky Mountain Geotechnical, was attempting to broaden the base of people in the firm who marketed its services.

The firm is a sole proprietorship with roughly 25 people. The proprietor was concerned about an overdependence on himself to bring in the majority of the firm's work. However, it's difficult not to get work when all 25 people are marketing.

In order to stimulate entrepreneurship, he created a program called "Marketing for Dollars," a takeoff on the old television show "Bowling for Dollars." He formed vertically sliced marketing teams within the firm. Each team had a senior engineer, a junior engineer, technicians, and clerical staff. However, a member of one team and a member of another team would *each* receive individual points for joint-effort marketing contributions that would help their respective team's total. After a period of time, the team with the greatest number of points was given a substantial cash prize to be divided at team members' discretion among themselves.

In addition, a person was selected as having made the greatest marketing contribution to the firm during that time period. (The selection was done by a cross section of people in the firm.) The winner was given an all-expense-paid weekend for two, anywhere within a 1,000-mile radius of Colorado Springs.

> Use caution in spurring internal competition. Entrepreneurship does go up. But internal competition can be destructive. Where competitive programs are more team-based, there is a better chance for win-win results. When any contribution is rewarded—and contributes to a team sense—performance improves.

The Innovator

Innovators, those creative but hard-to-manage risk-takers, are absolutely necessary in a firm that wants to be excellent. In order to maintain long-term excellence, a firm must:

- Identify innovators
- Create space for them
- Promote their survival in the firm

The income-producing side of firms tends to drain innovativeness, at least after a time. Innovators need a certain amount of looseness, the proverbial corner to play in, and periodical support. Still, you can't allow innovators to do whatever they wish whenever they wish. They can damage the productive earning capacity of your firm.

In the doing of an experiment, someone must volunteer to lead the effort, someone who has the *personal desire* to develop that particular idea.

> When an idea comes from management and is assigned, looseness and inventiveness may not survive. The person receiving the assignment has pressure to produce results, rather than tinker. Enthusiasm may be limited.

The goal is to simply allow ideas to flow from person to person in your firm. When someone commits energy to pursue an idea, you need to give that person enough freedom and time and encouragement to run with it.

A few years ago, an engineer in one of the Dames & Moore Texas offices devised a marketing strategy for attracting a great number of commissions for environmental studies on undersea acreage that was being leased to oil companies. The engineer set up a hospitality suite at the site at which the leases were being sold. Unique, essential information was posted in the suite, which attracted crowds of prospective clients. That initiative helped the firm secure dozens of environmental studies and air- and water-quality monitoring contracts.

McClelland Engineers Inc. has a unique materials development group in their Houston office. One of their materials development engineers—an innovator—was aboard ship on a project for clients in the North Sea. When reflecting on his experience during the long airplane trip home, he realized that one of the biggest problems his clients had in doing offshore geotechnical work was having to go through four separate testing processes with long "umbilical cords" from the ship to the ocean bottom.

He began thinking of ways for all four ocean-bottom soil-testing processes to be self-contained in a single unit. The ship could then drop just one device with a simple wire attachment. This device would float down to the right point on the bottom. It would be self-checking. It could bore its own holes and measure soil characteristics. And, it would even have self-contained computer capabilities.

From those innovators' reflections, McClelland Engineers Inc. developed what they call their Dolphin system. It provides a capability no one else in the world possesses. Through field observations, innovators such as this McClelland Engineers Inc. engineer sense areas of innovation that are required. They get reactions to their ideas from clients, from users, and from colleagues who work in the *operational* side. Then they create an internal proposal to gain management authorization to commit the time and resources of the testing group to develop the system. The firm provides the "laboratory."

Here is another example. Alan "Bubba" Jones, at Yearwood and Johnson in Nashville, Tennessee, was a recent graduate when he made use of his network of personal relationships to add new marketing dimensions to his firm's effort. He was an innovator.

He had "kin" throughout the part of Tennessee from which he came. And the firm allowed him time away from the office to return to his hometown area and gave him the encouragement to develop his "network." He strengthened established acquaintances, began building new ones, and brough significant leads and clients into the firm.

Jones had an interest. The firm supported that interest. Over a period of time, his capability in marketing began to match his enthusiasm. Several commissions, including several large hospital contracts, resulted.

One other unorthodox result of marketing innovation came from the Rocky Mountain Geotechnical's "Marketing for Dollars" program. A secretary was driving home one evening. At an intersection, a car crossing her path carried on its door the sign of a development company that was not then a client of the firm.

The secretary decided to follow the developer's car home. There she drew information from the developer about the nature of the projects he was doing. And she suggested that the developer really should be talking to some of the people in her firm.

The developer was amazed at the enthusiasm of the secretary and suggested that someone from Rocky Mountain Geotechnical give him a call. They did. And the firm received a lot of work from that developer.

Many people may *not* be thought of as innovators by senior staff. But staff members in support positions, such as secretaries or architectural interns, have opportunities to test other ideas:

- New equipment
- New management processes
- New marketing programs
- New incentive systems
- New concepts in CADD software

Such people can provide firms with unique advantages. In every case cited here, some time was provided to allow people to develop the ideas, to test them, and to see what could be done to follow through.

That's the kind of support a volunteer innovator needs.

Innovating Climates

There are three types of innovators.

All three types are essential for your firm to achieve an innovating climate and regular flow of new ideas. Without the presence of all three, production tends to be the total focus, with creative stagnation following.

First is the *product* innovator, a person with a passion for new products or services. This category includes people such as those found in McClelland Engineers Inc.'s materials development group, or the Princeton Energy Group's "Cool Bill." A product innovator has passion for his or her ideas and often has blinders on in other areas because of that passion.

The innovation *sponsor* is typically a former product or services innovator. He or she has moved up in the firm and is now a principal. That person no longer has the time for product development. Interests are shifted to business, marketing, and management pressures. But this person is in an excellent position to be supportive to the product innovator. He or she understands what has to happen, and is able to shield the product innovator from the pressures of the production side of the firm.

The innovation *hero* is an older leader, one who is a role model and who often leaves a myth in a firm because of the esteem for his or her earlier pioneering efforts. This type of person is often the founder of the firm.

Tony Aeck Jr. and Tony Aeck Sr. are both architects. Aeck Jr. graduated from architecture school and went to work in his father's Atlanta firm. Aeck Sr. allowed his son to attend many continuing education courses and to enjoy a relatively free rein to experiment with new ideas in the firm. The father made good use of the energy, optimism, and fresh ideas that his son carried over from his undergraduate and graduate school years.

Aeck Jr. experimented with passive solar energy systems; the firm became a pioneer in many project applications. He experimented with CADD; the firm was one of the first firms in Atlanta to have a full CADD system. Experimentation was also applied to other areas of the practice.

Essentially, Tony Aeck Sr. acted as an innovation *sponsor*, and Tony Jr. as a *product* innovator.

In BSW Architects in Tulsa, Chief Boyd is entrepreneurial. He enjoys and encourages innovations, but he does not actually *do* the writing of new computer programs.

However, Boyd created a sponsorship program in which any of the staff who saw an opportunity for new software—and wanted to develop it—received 50 percent support from the firm.

While staff members usually experimented on their own time, complete use of all facilities, including full use of all computer equipment and 50 percent pay for that time, was provided by the firm.

Software became part of the package provided by BSW Architects to other firms through a license with a CADD company. The staff who developed programs shared in royalties.

Boyd is a good example of an innovation *sponsor*. He created the environment and supplied the incentive and the emotional support that was necessary for innovators to flourish.

One of the greatest examples of an innovation hero is Frank Lloyd Wright. His Taliesin Foundation continues today. People continue to be driven by the ideals—and the stories—of Wright.

Innovation *heroes* establish legends over a long period of time. But the spirit they found and the advice they give to people who are current innovation sponsors lead to a host of younger product or services innovators.

If you are the principal of a firm, create time, support, and a perception that you *value* innovation. In a small firm, you will probably be a product innovator. Create a time and place for experimenting. In a larger firm, even of 10 or more, provide space, facilities, freedom, encouragement, and even incentives for product innovators. Heroes need only be available and visible to provide a model for others to emulate.

One important tenet about innovation climates is this:

A large *number* of attempts are required to produce successful innovation.

When pressure is applied for every innovation to be a success, failure is the typical result. The more time you go to bat in baseball, the more home runs you will get, regardless of your average. You simply need to increase the number of attempts to produce greater success. This means:

- A lot of hypothesizing
- Much testing
- Frequent refining
- A great deal of applying

Innovation sponsors need to provide opportunity. Innovators need to play, and to play *repeatedly*. Don't expect every attempt to provide results. But a few will, dramatically.

You rarely hear of the attempts that didn't work. But you can be certain that BSW Architects developed many computer programs that created nothing but frustration before they found one application that made all the failures seem worthwhile. And you can be sure that the Princeton Energy Group experienced a variety of failures that had to be laughed off before the breakthroughs brought success.

Communication

Three qualities of communication are critical to achieving excellence. Not surprisingly, all three foster entrepreneurial spirit. They are:

- Informality
- Intensity
- Opportunity

A continuous flow of *informal* communication is a first priority. This includes constant elbow-rubbing and frequent coming together. Communication in design firms must flow upward and downward, laterally and diagonally.

You need to maintain an intense, continuous form of contact. This can be facilitated through informal events, such as people having lunch with different people in the firm—just to get to know them better—and off-hour events of either a professional, social, or recreational nature.

Blount Corporation is a large contractor, headquartered in Montgomery, Alabama. Blount has rented such places as Callaway Gardens for annual meetings. The facility has golf courses, tennis courts, swimming pools, and a large number of meeting rooms. Blount flew people in from job sites all over the world. They ran shuttle buses 85 miles to and from the Atlanta airport to bring in employees and spouses. They brought in their entire permanent staff, top to bottom, for a three-day program.

The board of directors and top management had meetings on the weekend. On Monday, Tuesday, and Wednesday they conducted a very broad range of educational programs. Speakers at meals talked about communications, about motivation, about people sensitivity, and about memory. A multitude of day-long short courses were presented for all different levels in the company, from marketing to supervision. And in the evenings, entertainers were brought in from Hollywood and Las Vegas.

A lot of dialogue occurs among people in this type of a program. The president of Blount Brothers Corporation, the division of Blount Corporation that sponsored the event, indicated that while the program could cost them a quarter of a million dollars, the return on their investment—in terms of better communication and better capability in their company—has consistently been worth the investment.

How many firms make that level of commitment on a regular basis, even at a scale appropriate to their firm's size?

Vertical mixing is particularly essential. Excellent firms ensure that a lot of informal vertical mixing occurs. In a firm of three, vertical mixing happens naturally. But in a firm of even 12 or 20, vertical mixing tends to give way to the observance of hierarchy and informal communication can break down.

The climate in your firm should facilitate intense arguing and negotiating, in all directions. A junior person and a principal should be able to argue with one another. Principals can always fire the junior person. Yet the climate must be such that they can openly argue in a direct and unrestricted manner.

This is the kind of open communication that's necessary for ideas to flourish, to be freely exchanged and debated, but not be crushed.

Intensive dialogue also creates energy in the office environment.

This is the kind of negotiation that happens in a healthy family. If it does not occur, and if grievances are swallowed, families can end up with runaway kids or parents.

A strong family clings together, but it also argues together. It's a process of hammering out roles and ideas and values. The question of authority of a parent or of a son or daughter or of grandparents becomes moot. Success hinges on each person's ability to negotiate in an intense, direct way, sometimes for hours and even into the night.

> Excellent firms do, and must, have this same consistent, ongoing intensity of communication. Less time should be spent on memos and more on dialogue.

Most excellent firms also sponsor occasional events to facilitate even more dialogue. Some have an annual retreat. Weekend continuing education events are increasingly common. Many have quarterly reviews that involve the entire firm. And still others sponsor purely social events, such as ski or beach weekends.

One of the firms mentioned earlier, McClelland Engineers Inc. in Houston, is a 750-person firm. Bram McClelland, the founder, has achieved significant stature among his colleagues in the profession. His is probably one of the top two offshore geotechnical firms in the world.

Yet young associates feel free to challenge him. Several were convinced that their overhead multipliers, which affect the fees in their proposals, were excessive. They wanted reductions in the firm's general overhead costs. They virtually stormed McClelland's office, had a very intense dialogue, and caused major cutbacks in general overhead spending.

The key here was that the middle-level staff of the firm was *able* to challenge the head of this large firm. McClelland is a successful person with a strong personality. However, he is open to *listening* to his people.

The quality of communication in that firm is such that people can take him on without fear of losing their jobs, and with an intense desire to bring about a positive change in the firm.

Another firm we have referred to before, Dames & Moore, was conducting a partner's meeting. The firm brings their 100 or so partners together once every year or two from offices around the world. This is an expensive undertaking, much like the Blount Corporation's annual meeting.

At one particular meeting, two of the firm's four United States regional managers entered into a heated discussion with the managing partner of one of their major offices. The office manager was talking to his immediate supervisor and to another regional manager.

They disputed a policy that was being debated among the partners. And their dispute continued through the entire evening, until two o'clock in the morning.

A lot of stress occurs in those kinds of disagreements. But the climate was healthy enough that the partners could argue intensely and at length with each other, regardless of their roles and level of authority in the firm.

If those kinds of arguments were never *able* to occur, a lot of intense negative feelings would build. Pent-up emotion breeds anger, not excellence.

One of the tangibles you can look for in an excellent firm are *physical supports* that expand the opportunity for communication. Examples include:

- Chalkboards or flip charts in offices
- Places where people can meet and talk
- Spaces for drinking coffee
- Erasable or postable information surfaces in shared spaces

These opportunity vehicles, because of their multiple-person use, promote communication in a firm.

Rocky Mountain Geotechnical has a "leads wall." All leads brought to the office (such as by the secretary who drove after the developer or from inquiries made by a variety of prospects) are posted on the wall. The display has five levels: initial leads; qualified leads; live visits made; proposals submitted; and proposals won or lost.

What's the significance of the wall?

The wall provides a visible, *physical* entity that facilitates increased levels of open communication—in this case, about marketing.

All 23 people in the firm meet weekly. They review the status of all leads being pursued. They review the status of all proposals pending. And they enter new leads.

When they see a growing need for new leads, they spend more time looking for them. If they have a fair number of leads, but not enough of them are being pursued, they also adjust. The wall encourages them to guide their marketing efforts.

Their "Marketing for Dollars" program also has giant visible "thermometers"—modeled after the United Way goal display thermometers. As the teams earn points bringing in new work, they can see the impacts of their efforts.

Part of your consideration in creating increased communication opportunities is *proximity*. Staff workspaces and communication support should be close to one another.

The down side of closeness is that people sometimes need to be alone to work on a project. Technically-oriented people often seek isolation. However, in the normal flow of events, the greater the proximity and the greater the mixing, the more intense the communication and the greater the health of your firm.

For example: HTB Architects is a large multi-discipline firm based in Oklahoma City. It has a variety of satellite offices, including Tulsa, New Orleans, Washington, D.C., and a number of other cities. One of the policies in the firm is: "All work must be done at the *local* site."

While the firm may have 30 or 40 people in the Washington, D.C. office, specialists from other offices, many of whom are located in their headquarters in Oklahoma City, are required to work on Washington projects in Washington. Those specialists move to Washington, for two days or two weeks or two months.

All work is done on site.

The project team typically has certain long-term, permanent members. Others, who work only on interim portions of the project, are in close physical proximity when their segment of the project is being addressed. They work on the job *together*, rubbing elbows in the same space.

Motivating Systems

One motivating system which supports the building of entrepreneurial spirit is one which labels, names, or gives awards for results of improved communication. Motivators tend to oblige greater *individual initiative* and a more spirited feeling of entrepreneurship.

For example, societies confer fellowships. "FAIA," or "Fellow of the AIA," designates significant contribution in design, in community contributions, or in any one of a variety of defined categories. It's a system that recognizes and encourages excellence in the society's members.

Some firms have think tanks. Members of a think tank carry a certain esteem in having been selected. The esteem, in turn, prompts entrepreneurial behavior.

Some firms provide new business venture capital, developmental money, to people who have an idea. They act on the belief that those ideas will lead to positive results. Again, *esteem* is attached to that developmental behavior.

The materials development group at McClelland Engineers Inc., for instance, developed Ram Velocity Monitor (RVM). This unique instrument measures the actual velocity of the head on a pile driver. It solves a major problem that is shared by both pile driver contractors and owners who *pay* for pile drivers. They can now know the *actual* force being delivered to the pile.

Because pile driving payment often equates to actual results, both parties wish to monitor the efficiency of the pile driving equipment. The ability to accurately measure the actual productivity of the equipment at a given time has generally been suspect. So, McClelland Engineers Inc. developed a unique product.

Engineers who were in the laboratory and in the field began observing this need. From their observations, they wrote a description of their idea to see if their peers would give support and if they could gain client sponsorship. When they receive encouragement, they apply directly to top management for funding.

It's a system for awarding venture capital to new ideas. Consequently, it encourages development of new ideas. And the motivating process adds esteem to applied R&D innovation.

A Tulsa, Oklahoma, firm known as Architectural Collective, is led by Leon Ragsdale. It has an interesting structure.

Originally, it was a traditional architectural firm. Then, the principals found a need for additional interior design capability. Eventually, interior design staff was added, but as a *separate* firm.

Then came the need for better furniture. A separate furniture group was formed. The new group could sell furniture directly or it could acquire furniture for the architecture and interior groups' clients. The new venture became another extended service for the architecture and design clients, but as a separate company.

The principals then found that many of their commercial projects needed custom sculpture and artwork for lobbies. Many artisans in the area also needed a "shelter." *Another* company was created. It could generate tailored artwork for commercial projects.

The commercial projects alone didn't keep the artisans fully occupied, so they opened *another* company, in which the artisans could teach art classes, and sell their artifacts.

Then, the need for construction management grew. Ragsdale brought in a semiretired contractor who worked with the architectural firm, but did so by forming a construction management (CM) company. The new venture began developing its own CM work, which could also be done for other architectural firms.

The Architectural Collective was the motivating system. Each new venture led to the creation of a separate company. The system was decentralized to keep it entrepreneurial. Each company had to make it on its own. The companies were connected. They did support one another. But they also worked independently.

Excellent firms build and then nurture an environment that encourages and supports entrepreneurial spirit. In this chapter, we discussed key ways to achieve entrepreneurial environment.

> Decentralize. Keep your staff close to the action. The closer staff feel to the hub, and the more connected they feel to the organization, the more enthusiastic and creative they will be.

> Encourage and support innovators. Keep the flow of new ideas coming by creating an innovating climate.

> Make an open flow of communication a high priority. Encourage all forms of communication. Informal elbow rubbing and intense arguing, for example, are necessary ingredients to an entrepreneurial environment and should be unrestrained.

> Reward individual initiative.

You can readily implement the concepts in this chapter to increase personal feelings of individuality and entrepreneurship in your firm. These methods can also cause your firm to be a much more exciting place to work.

CHAPTER 5

TAKING GOOD CARE OF YOUR PEOPLE

The people of your firm are its foundation. One of the qualities consistently found in excellent firms is a genuine commitment to help people in the firm to be productive and then reward them for it.

Dos Instead of Don'ts

It is basic to human nature to respond better to positive than to negative suggestion and reinforcement. It is just common sense in managing for excellence to encourage and reward the productive actions and attitudes of people who work for you—to put dos ahead of don'ts. Yet it isn't as common as you might imagine.

> Think about *communicating* dos in your firm—in ways that range from signs around the office to well-broadcast policies.

For example, BSW Architects in Tulsa has a policy that says to its employees, "Do develop computer software." Even if the software development is accomplished with some of the firm's resources, the developers receive royalties.

Rocky Mountain Geotechnical's "Marketing for Dollars" program, which was talked about in the previous chapter, encourages staffers to look for leads. Everyone in the firm receives rewards for bringing in leads, for pursuing projects, and for developing letters and proposals for projects.

When someone in the Blount Brothers Corporation, whether contractor or engineer, becomes a vice president, the company sends the new officers to a Harvard Business School summer course for two months. It's a matter of policy.

These kinds of dos support actions intended to develop and promote the person and the firm.

Feedback is another form of do. Several firms have sponsored programs that feature performance feedback techniques for their employees.

Arctic Engineers, in Anchorage, Alaska, sponsored a three-day professional development program for the entire firm. Part of it focused on marketing; part of it on management. At the end, the employees exchanged candid observations about each other's performance in the firm. This included staff-to-staff, principal-to-staff, and staff-to-principal.

Feedback is structured to emphasize the *positive*:

> "Here are some things you do that I value most. But also, here are some more things you could do to expand your value."

The Big Picture

A firm performs better when everyone in it understands the total mission. A firm really owes it to the staff to communicate what the big picture looks like. Even in three- and four-person firms, attitudes will be self-limiting unless those few people understand how their jobs add to the total mission of the firm.

> "I was hired to do wall sections and drafting. That's all I do."

This is a typical expression of tunnel vision. Even marketing people sometimes get blocked by their business-development viewpoints and don't think about important firm-wide objectives, such as quality control or long-term goals.

A bookkeeper, for example, could receive guidance on which information in "the books" might provide feedback. Certain projects could be consistent money losers; marketing or project management effort could be shifted in response to the bookkeeper's information.

Everyone in an excellent firm shares the big picture. What every employee does is a piece of the whole.

Some firms are afraid that if their people know the big picture, they'll "give away the store" by telling friends who work for competing firms. The attitude reflects mistrust.

A 20- to 25-person firm in Houston had three principals, some project managers, professional staff, and support staff. Employees were asked by consultants for suggestions on how the firm could increase its effectiveness. People talked about things they enjoyed and didn't enjoy about the firm.

One project manager was quite unhappy. He had just learned that his unit had overrun its latest project budget by a huge margin. He felt terrible—and frustrated. He had never been told what the project budget was. "The principals here don't share financial information."

In this firm, the principals shared neither the budget in dollars, nor the work hours allocated to do the project. They figured, "If the project people know the budget, they'll know we are obviously taking a fortune from the firm for ourselves. Or, if we tell them the budgeted time, they'll be able to work backwards and still figure out that we are taking a fortune for ourselves."

"And if we tell them we budgeted 30 hours to complete one phase, they'll *spend* all 30 hours."

The project managers in the Houston firm had no idea what the budget was at the outset, and they received no further information as the project progressed to let them know if they were within budget. They had no chance to make adjustments during the project. They learned only afterwards that they had overrun the budget.

Space Design International (SDI), a successful interiors firm headquartered in Cincinnati, Ohio, does a variety of corporate, retail, and institutional projects in the central and southeast part of the country.

A few years ago, SDI's marketing director devoted a wall in her office for posting leads, similar in purpose to the Rocky Mountain Geotechnical's, which was mentioned in Chapter 4. The wall was divided with horizontal bands into five levels:

> First, when a member of the firm heard about a potential project, an index card was filled out and taped to the lowest level, closest to the floor. This was for hearsay, unqualified leads. Information on the card included client and project names, phone numbers, and names of staff who had relationships with people in the client organization.

Then, the marketing director and other staff members went to work qualifying those leads. Were they real or not? The staff set up appointments. If the leads were real and the project was available to the firm, the index card moved up to the next level—"qualified leads."

The third level was reached after a first live visit by the most appropriate staff member.

The fourth level indicated that second and third visits had been conducted and that letters and proposals were submitted. The firm was *courting* the client.

The fifth level consisted of final presentation or proposal.

At any given level, the prospective job could fade or drop out. It could turn out not to be a qualified lead. The marketers might have a first meeting with a client, feel poor chemistry, and decide against pursuing the job further.

The key here is that every week the firm's entire staff, roughly 24 to 28 people, gathered in the marketing office. The entire wall in that office was set up to show what was happening in the firm's marketing effort. By sharing all of that information, *everyone* knew what kinds of projects were being pursued.

Everyone began to think and talk marketing.

A typical benefit involved one of the secretaries, who had previously been the secretary for Butler Aviation in Cincinnati, where she had arranged to have all the executive planes ready for their owners. As a result, she personally knew all the executives in Cincinnati who flew. The firm's knowledge of her network surfaced during the marketing meeting when she offered to call the head of a corporation listed on the board.

In summary, open communication leads to positive, productive action:

The more your staff knows about your project, the more they will take responsibility for completing it within budget and in response to your client's needs.

The more your employees understand your firm's goals, the more they can and will support them.

Investment in People

Training is vital if you want strong performance from your staff. This means you'll need to spend dollars and commit staff time.

When firms are busy, nonbillable time is lost profits.

Sending an employee to a two-day course is an investment. Your expenditure is not limited to the tuition and expenses. It also includes the amount of time that your employee could have billed, and what your staff member costs you in salary and benefits.

Your investment will hopefully bring benefits in the future.

One of the common denominators of all excellent organizations, from IBM to Xerox to McDonalds to Boeing, is a consistent and continued commitment to training.

Another dimension to investing in people is that once you have invested in training, you need to give your people some freedom to *use* their skills and knowledge.

To give people marketing training, for example, and then not have them in contact with clients, doesn't help your firm achieve a return on its investment. If you give people training in computer-aided designs and don't have a CADD system, the training is wasted.

The first issue in training is *relevance*, identifying the areas in which your staff wants training. You can talk about a multitude of topics in which all should take courses. But if you have to assign priorities, you must ask what issues are most pressing and what do people have the *greatest* need to learn?

For example, during the recession of the early 1980s, design professionals had tremendous needs for marketing. As the recession ended, firms became busier. Needs still exist for marketing, but they're more oriented for long-term issues, such as market research on the next two, three or four years and larger-scale strategies (rather than just chasing each potential project).

Many training courses now include topics, such as productivity, time management, project management, CADD, financial management, and negotiating fees.

One of the best ways of identifying needs is to listen.

If you begin to hear patterns of curiosity or interest, you may have identified the topics that could be covered in courses for your entire firm. For instance, most of the employees of Arctic Engineers were interested in improving their personal productivity. Such a course was brought to the firm.

The training already discussed is individual. Topics can include personal productivity, marketing, project management, and a number of other areas.

The larger picture of training includes training in a sequence. This leads to career development.

Some new skills training can be done through courses. Some can be done with on-the-job training. For a period of time, two employees may be doing the job that one could have done. However, two can later do the job simultaneously, on separate projects.

It's a way of investing extra time now to reap a greater payoff later.

In terms of long-term career development, few firms take the time to ask people, even for 45 minutes per person per year, where they would like to be professionally in a few years. Once your employees' goals have been identified, you can help to achieve them.

This information could influence a person's job assignment. It certainly would influence the training you'd organize, whether done by on-the-job training or formal courses.

Giving people training, autonomy, career development, and opportunity to grow professionally leads to a sense of becoming a real part of your firm. However, higher level jobs need to be available.

One of the successes mentioned earlier was Alan "Bubba" Jones of Yearwood and Johnson. Over a four- to six-year period, Jones began to manage small teams and brought in several leads for new projects. The firm allowed him to move up. He now manages a significant segment of the firm.

Your firm has to provide space for people like Jones to develop. If they grow beyond the opportunities your firm offers, they'll need to find another job and you'll need to find other employees.

The Vickery Partnership is a small firm in Charlottesville, Virginia. Robert Vickery is a professor at the University of Virginia and a practicing architect. He started a firm and enjoys a dual occupation.

The firm prospered and built a cadre of people. Within that group of employees were several bright young professionals who had a promising future. Vickery needed to decide if those architects were going to be a part of the firm, or if it was going to remain the Vickery Partnership. Or whether the firm should change, so that as these people grew in their capabilities they could become an *integral* part of the firm.

The firm, at even an 8- to 10-person size, had sponsored training. A weekend program in marketing was conducted for everyone. Many employees also had taken management courses. The firm no longer was simply an extension—in the atelier tradition—of Bob Vickery. It had developed a team of leaders. Vickery was open to shared leadership, and people in the firm had an opportunity to grow into it.

As their professionalism developed, their roles in the firm also evolved. They did not work themselves out of a job. In fact, the firm's name now reflects four partners, one of which is Vickery. It also now employs 40 people.

> The sense of ownership—not just legal, but emotional ownership—of people *all* taking responsibility for marketing, for design, and for production, produces the power of a shared system.

Vickery's is an example of a firm giving its younger people an opportunity to develop their careers and mature, with the security of knowing that the firm will evolve with them.

Rewards and Awards

Employees who do well with new training, who develop new skills, and who mature in the firm should be rewarded. These rewards can be:

- Money, as in Rocky Mountain Geotechnical's "Marketing for Dollars"
- Promotions, as in the case of Jones at Yearwood and Johnson
- Ownership, as in the case of the young architects of the Vickery Partnership who became partners

Excellent firms know the value of giving awards. They do it often. Sometimes the awards are tacky; sometimes they are sensitive and ingenious.

In 1974, the AIA sponsored a continuing education program on the *Michelangelo*, an Italian luxury liner. It was an eight-day cruise, with professional seminars conducted en route.

One of the participants was a young Boston architect who was sent by his firm. He said that he had been working extraordinarily hard for the last few months on a significant project. About the time that he met the project deadline, the firm said to him,

"Why don't you and your wife go off on this cruise for eight days? There are a couple of interesting courses. You can pick up a great suntan. And you can enjoy some interesting sights. When you come back, you'll be ready to return to work."

That was a very sensitive, very personal type of award.

> One of the shortcomings associated with awards is that people will not sell themselves to you. However, they will give themselves to you "for a ribbon."

People tend to attach more *meaning* to trophies, certificates, and to symbolic awards than they do to cash.

Some businesses have their first dollar bill framed and hung over the cash register. Many more have certificates, such as college diplomas, license certificates, awards, fellowship in their professional society, or trophies on their walls. People take pride in these symbols of achievement. They are also long-lasting.

Some of the symbols cost your firm very few dollars. Some cost quite a bit more. Yet, it is the *symbol*, not its dollar value that produces the greatest impact.

Residuals Management Technology (RMT) is a firm headquartered in Madison, Wisconsin. It is about half engineers and half scientists. RMT works largely with hazardous waste in industrial hygiene. It has predominately industrial clients. Clean air, clean water, and clean earth is its focus.

The director of marketing set up a large-scale awards program. One of the most significant awards turned out to be the Fog Light Award, named for the circumstances of its inception.

A proposal was due in Milwaukee. The firm's secretary had to drive to Milwaukee through several hours of fog to deliver it. The proposal *was* delivered. And the firm received the contract. For her "above and beyond effort," the secretary received the company's first Fog Light Award. (It was a set of fog lights that she was able to use on her car.)

Ever since, the firm has awarded the Fog Light Award for effort that is truly extraordinary.

Many RMT staffers receive certificates, such as certificates of merit, for a variety of performances in marketing. They also receive stars—old-fashioned colored and gold stars like children used to get on grade school papers.

It's often the funny little awards that give people incentive to go out and work a bit more.

Firms can give titles that have more meaning and dignity than "drafter" or "technician." A title that suggests one is "a nothing" promotes low-level attitudes toward performance and contribution. If you think other people regard you as nothing, you'll behave to prove them right.

If a title suggests that the employee is moving up in the firm, then the behavior of the well-titled person may sharpen accordingly:

- Senior Designer
- Project Document Fulfillment Officer
- Director of Administration
- Vice President, Marketing
- Senior Vice President, Technical Quality
- Chief Engineer

In some firms, "Associate" means that you have a share of ownership. In others you don't. Ownership in a firm is tenuous, at best, because service firms aren't generally worth much. "Book value" in a service organization is a small fraction of what a firm may be worth to its members.

But, Associate is *recognition*. The title can add a little status on a business card. Many people enjoy titles such as Designer or Chief Designer or Senior Designer instead of staff or back-room employee. It lets them feel as though they have accomplished something above and beyond the paycheck they are drawing.

And, people will go to the ends of the earth for that kind of appreciation.

Small Groups

The value of small groups first came up in the discussion of sidestreaming in Chapter 2. For almost any task, small groups tend to work more effectively than larger groups. People relate better to one another and to a project in teams of four or teams of six, than they do in teams of 50 or teams of 90.

When working in small project teams, mix people of different functions (such as design, drafting, specification writing, and management) and different disciplines (such as architecture, interior design, landscape architecture, site engineering, and structures). All of them gain different perspectives.

While employees work on a job, they also have in-between time, such as coffee breaks and lunch hours. That's where the different perspectives develop. The mixing produces synergistic contributions that are achievable in almost no other way.

For instance, one of the team members may be in R&D. As that person listens to two or three others from design or production, the discussion may spark an idea that can lead to development of a whole new activity.

A food-service consulting firm, Cini-Little International, frequently uses focus groups at the front end of a project. Reviewed are the design, the square footages, early plans, quality of the furnishings, quality of ambience, kind of food-service menus, and type of actual food to be offered. A tremendous synergy occurs in small (eight- to twelve-person) focus groups. The result is a better-quality project and a shorter completion period.

Many of the larger firms that sponsor a regular flow of training, such as O'Brien-Gere Engineering, Dames & Moore, and McClelland Engineers Inc., conduct their training at a central site.

In Dames & Moore's case, it selects a site near the center of the country, because of the large number of offices. McClelland Engineers Inc.'s programs occur near McClelland Center, its headquarters building in Houston, Texas. O'Brien-Gere Engineering's programs occur near its Syracuse, New York headquarters.

Employees from different offices come together. The training programs are also limited to small groups, typically of 20 to 30 employees.

A lot of mixing occurs among people who don't normally see each other.

The Extended Family

Some observers perceive that in our society, the institutions of school and church are no longer as strong as they were 100 or 200 or 300 years ago.

Many of our personal focuses are centered on our families, our community, our neighbors, and our hobbies. But for many people, their firm and their profession are the core around which much of their life is built.

Many of us work 12, 14, or 15 hour days on a regular 6-day-a-week basis. The reason isn't just low profitability and having to put in more time. Rather, it's a way of life that is an extension of our natural inclinations, desires, and interests.

Many excellent firms, accordingly, try to integrate a certain amount of personal activity with professional activity.

When the Blount Corporation rented Callaway Gardens, many spouses were brought to the Gardens, and programs were conducted for them too. Many spouses also had their own professions and so attended programs that taught particular skills they could use in their own fields.

Social events were held in the evenings. Singers and entertainment groups were brought in from Las Vegas and Hollywood. It became an event a family could look forward to. It was part of the company. And it was part of their *life* in the company.

Rocky Mountain Geotechnical has ski weekends in the Rockies. It rents one or more chalets. And the whole firm will get together for a weekend, to ski and eat and be together.

Tiller, Butner and Rosa, a 25- to 30-person architectural firm in Montgomery, Alabama, periodically charters a riverboat on the Alabama River, which flows through Montgomery. They have great parties.

Some of the parties are also attended by clients. But, some are only for the employees and their families.

Taking good care of your people isn't limited to the time spent between nine and five. You should help them understand the total picture of your firm. Think *beyond* your firm's immediate needs and extend your focus to their career development. People may then develop upwards in your firm, working with leaders on a personal basis.

Offer the kind of training to your staff that will allow them to grow professionally. Make sure your firm is in a position to grow with them.

As growth is made, as achievements are realized, you need to give awards, recognition, titles, and certificates, in a variety of ways.

Finally, think about your staff members' development as people, not just in terms of their professional skills and their careers. Encourage them to get to know one another as individuals, including the people they care about outside the office.

CHAPTER 6

PUTTING VALUES AT THE CORE

Many design firms simply exist. The people at the top have personal values and beliefs, but they're not *expressed* in the workplace or shared with the firm. Consequently, the firm has no *consistent core* around which to build a consistent and powerful practice.

To articulate your firm's values, you must find answers to these questions:

- Why have we established our firm
- What kind of practice do we wish to be
- What do we believe is most important to a good practice
- What qualities do few other firms have that we want to have

With a core of values, decisions reinforce one another. Everyone's energy can be better focused. Regardless of size, your firm will be more consistently successful.

One way of expressing these values is described by a time management consultant of the Insight Company as "Unifying Principles." Examples of unifying principles in your design firm could include:

- Responsiveness to both clients and others
- Being at the *forefront* of professional knowledge
- Highest quality of contract documents
- Contribution to a beautiful environment
- Personal learning and growth for all employees
- Strong physical conditioning for all employees

This set of values becomes the *foundation* for an excellent firm.

Qualitative, not Quantitative

Values should *not* deal with quantitative issues. Profits and money objectives are necessary. However, they don't reflect "why" or "how." The world provides many opportunities to make money. Numbers don't reflect *why* you've selected your particular practice.

Values reflect beliefs. As such, they address qualities.

> Excellence is not quantitative. It can be achieved by firms of any size.

Varney Sexton Lunsford Aye is a long-established 30- to 50-person firm in Phoenix, Arizona. Ed Varney is in his 70s and had done mostly institutional work, such as schools and correctional and health care facilities, for over 40 years.

One of the firm's goals is to maintain design excellence. The principals want the expression of that excellence to be a *firm-wide* level of design quality, not individually varying results. On the other hand, the principals also don't want to step on the creativity of individuals.

They want their firm's design to not just be "George's design" this time and "Sally's design" next time. They want a firm-wide design contributed by George and Sally, both of whom would have freedom to express their creativity within the larger framework.

One of the programs established by the firm, as a result, has been a special design review process. This review process, unlike the juries used in universities, is constructive. Everyone in the firm can participate, including the clerical staff and other support people. The reviews are often done during off hours, such as lunchtime or after 5 P.M., so that all can participate.

The principals set up a system for gathering feedback about the design:

The designer presents information about the project.

Questions are answered for clarification.

The participants caucus in groups of two or three. Feedback must be structured using the following guidelines:

- Describe the feature you like *best* about the design; indicate *why* you like it
- Describe the feature you like *least*, and why
- Repeat, until you've listed all positive and negative features
- You must have an equal number of each
- Comments must be specific and descriptive (for example, "I like your use of red brick because it blends with the original building" is better than "I like your use of materials.")

Feedback is provided to the designer, moving from group to group until each group runs out of comments. While all changes to the design are decided by the *designer*, not the groups, the process leads to consistent *refinement* of the initial design.

Because of the usefulness of the process, designers request reviews two to three times during schematics and once during design development.

What about "bottom-line" results?

Refinements result from that process every time. Significant improvements are especially evident after two or three iterations. The designer achieves a consistently better product.

The firm *values* a consistently high quality of design and they then take steps to *achieve* that result.

Mudano Associates in Clearwater, Florida, established a preventive maintenance program. Paraphrased, here are the values that gave rise to the program.

We care about our clients and our projects, as do most firms. But our caring extends *beyond* the immediate project completion for which we're paid.

When we design a project, when we administer construction, and when the client occupies the building, we don't wave the client farewell. That's the *start* of our commitment!

We will stay *with* that building, every few months, for years. We'll take care of additions. We'll take care of renovations. We'll talk with the client about adjustments. We'll take care of energy conservation. We'll adjust it for computer adaptability.

As times change, the firm is committed to stay with the facility on a long-term basis. Again, a value of this firm is long-term commitment to each client and client organization. They structure their operating systems, such as preventive maintenance, to help them achieve that particular value.

Mission

Everyone in your firm needs to accept your firm's values. When they do, they'll begin to share in your firm's mission.

A drafter taking a job can say,

> "Well, I can be a drafter in Firm A, or a drafter in Firm B, or a drafter in Firm C. It's all the same, really."

> A typist can type for A or B or C. A project manager can manage projects for A or B or C.

What do you do to *differentiate* your firm from others and also instill the values of your firm in your people?

"Mission" is a good word; it suggests a quality of passion. When people join a firm that has a mission, rather than just taking a job, they're joining a mission. They need to commit themselves to that mission and put their personal *energy* into that mission.

> Your firm's mission should be known to all new people coming into your firm as the "real goal of your firm."

An example of values that could inspire people would be: No sacrifice of quality.

You might say in your firm that, "You're going to do it *right*, regardless." Every time people talk compromisingly about the quality of drawings, of reports, of solutions, of paper to use or the prints to produce, you can go back to your statement and say, "No, we *won't* sacrifice the quality. It must be done right." Your commitment can inspire everybody to do their tasks at a "step-beyond" level.

Beliefs

Seven sets of beliefs are associated with values and mission—and their power to inspire people in a firm. None of the seven are new to you; one by one, each has been discussed as a quality of excellence in the preceding five chapters.

They are reviewed here because they are areas from which value statements can be derived and, shortly, implemented. The seven sets of beliefs are:

- Be the best
- Details are as important as the big picture
- People should be respected as individuals
- Extra service is part of excellence
- Innovators are valuable
- Informal company culture works
- Growth and profits are important

The first of the beliefs that inspire is what is called "be the best." That means setting a standard for all aspects of your practice that is a step *above* the equivalent standard of all other firms.

You don't have to be the biggest firm. But within the range of activities and services you decide to provide, yours needs to be the best.

One firm where being the best is a value is Glave, Newman, Anderson (GNA), in Richmond, Virginia, a 25- to 40-person firm known by colleagues, competitors, and clients as a "quality firm." Beyond being a competitor, they are a respected firm. When other firms compete against them for jobs, they often say, "If we beat GNA, we've beaten a good firm."

What constitutes being a "good" firm?

When energy conservation was a major concern in the 1970s, GNA quickly had people become skilled in passive solar design. Energy conservation was built into their designs. Many other firms paid only lip service to the issue and never developed extensive capabilities.

A few years ago, the Virginia Chapter of the AIA sponsored a course in management, dealing with the quality of environment in the firms. GNA's entire firm attended. They all designed and wore smocks, as a kind of firm-wide uniform. It was the only firm that displayed such pride. It was the only firm that closed its doors, so that everyone in the company could attend.

As use of CADD expanded, GNA was one of the first firms to become involved. Whenever a trend suggests an important new movement in the profession, GNA has firm members learn about it and weaves the new development into their practice.

While GNA isn't *always* the first in town to offer a new feature, the firm consistently makes investments in new capabilities. The commitment is a value—a unifying principle—a particular position that this firm takes that affects its management decisions, its training of staff, and its service.

Another belief needed if excellence is to be achieved is that details—and attention to them—are as important as the big picture.

When a client asks for a redesigned lobby or a waste treatment facility, he or she is really asking you to solve a problem. Your effort has to be carried all the way through, and that means details.

An example mentioned earlier involved Rodney Wright and The Hawkweed Group. It discovered that the rocks that had been sitting outside during the winter were cold. When they were put in the rockbed, they produced *cold* air during the entire first winter. A successful passive solar design had to be carried through to a level of detail that included the temperature of the rocks being used for thermal mass, as they were stored during construction.

Many firms have tremendous pride in what they call their "50- to 60-year-old crowd." These are generally people who have been in the construction field for a long time. They form a cadre of senior field people that help the firm make sure that the implementation of the design—and adjustments that have to be made in the field—are made at a high level of quality.

The Varney Sexton Lunsford Aye firm has such a group of construction administrators. It has a special pride *because* of its experience. It is a "crack team."

Many firms put some of their younger staff people in the field. They're less expensive, but they don't have the construction *experience*. A firm such as Varney Sexton Lunsford Aye will tend to deliver a project that is very close to the design intent *because* of the attention to detail they achieve with their senior people in the field.

Seeing people as objects necessary to the completion of projects leads to attitudes of "putting in time" and "a job is a job."

> Respecting people as individuals is a value that inspires staff to greater initiative and effort.

The Birmingham, Alabama firm of Evan Terry Architects is a 14- to 18-person firm. It has been a successful firm for many years. In fact, some of the staff have been with Evan Terry Architects for 20 to 30 years.

One of the men had a serious heart condition which disabled him for months. Though the firm isn't a giant, and struggles when carrying an extra load, the person received reasonable compensation for the *entire* time he was out. The time period was well beyond any defined benefits, beyond even what the employee would have reasonably expected. The firm was saying, "We take care of our people."

In a fairly large number of design firms, some of the senior people have, over the years, become active alcoholics. (It happens much more often than you'd expect.)

Yet, when one of the people, after years of working with clients and encountering continual stress in working issues in the firm, becomes an alcoholic, does the firm throw the person out? Or, do they say, "Look, it's time! You *must* go to a treatment center. We'll pay the costs. And we'll cover your salary while you're being treated. But you *must* be treated."

Firms show caring when people have individual problems. They show caring about people when they regularly sponsor training and development. Respect includes encouraging people to achievements that are *independent* of the firm and may even have to do with caring for and about their families.

The result of this attitude—caring—is the application of a core value about people that will make your firm more than just a place to work.

Here is the notion of going a step beyond.

An average level of performance exists in all professions, including the design professions. This standard is often referred to as the "typical architectural service," the "typical engineering service," or the "typical interior design service." The standard is defined by the performance of most firms and, as a result, sets client expectations for a "reasonable" level of service. (In fact, the same approach is used legally, in liability suits, to determine whether or not a professional has followed "*acceptable* professional standards.")

What does it take to go *beyond* that?

An excellent firm should exceed the levels of performance set by most firms. Higher levels of performance should be seen in as many categories of practice as possible.

In the grouping of firms that constitutes the Architectural Collective, in Tulsa, the various firms are able to provide a range of services that many other firms cannot provide. The sculptors and artists, for example, allow the collective to provide services that few other single-source firms have the capability to do.

BSW Architects, also in Tulsa, uses its computers to go a step beyond. They provide telephone monitoring services for nursing homes. They provide computerized land analysis for their developer clients, to give them support in developing their projects more prudently, even *before* they acquire the land. They help them do analyses of sites so that they can come out with an even *better* solution than they had originally envisioned. Again, the costs paid for these added services are small, compared to the benefit received by the client.

Every design firm needs to ask:

- What are the norms that we're practicing now
- What else could we do that would take it a step beyond

Your firm has to establish an *expectation for innovation*. All employees should constantly look for new ways to do their jobs better, and managers should look for ways to reward innovators.

Professionals talk about having innovators in the firm. Yet, in most respects, they seek "good support people," not innovation.

This excellence-producing ideal encourages a variety of people in the firm to be constantly thinking about new ways of doing things, about upgrading, and about refining. From basic support to your highest technical level, a large variety of innovations *can* occur to improve the way things are done in your firm.

Arctic Engineers, the Anchorage, Alaska, firm, is a company of innovators. If a project has been done once, it typically is not too interested in doing it a second time.

It constantly looks at new technologies. In fact, when a new wastewater treatment digester system was developed in Germany, Arctic arranged to be the only licensed distributor in the United States. The firm has also begun developing unique ways of *adapting* the process, as it applies it to different projects.

Virtually all of the individuals in this firm are innovators. They like to modify, adapt, design, and redesign in their own way. Rather than having a "harmonious" group work fluidly together, the firm's environment resembles isolated sparks.

However, the general perception about that firm is that when you have an unusual challenge that needs to be met, this is the firm you turn to.

Your firm needs to be a *relaxed* place for working, even if you have offices of great size. Most firms having fewer than 10 people are going to be relatively informal. However, even small firms can become too "tidy." The principal, as the sole proprietor, may set himself or herself a little above the others. Firms of even six or seven can become a little too formal to achieve the *fluidity* needed for achieving excellence.

Some firms of 12 have been known to pass out memos, rather than sitting down and talking with one another.

Maintaining an informal process demands time. However, the informality provides the *glue* that keeps people together. People feel as though they really are important. And performance improves accordingly.

Informality is not simply an open-door policy. It's the reality that people *can*, in fact, drop in at any time. Sometimes, the principal of the informal firm may also be out visiting among the staff.

The final belief is that one needs to complete a job not in order to "make a killing," but to come in within the budget so that a reasonable profit results.

Your profit must be sufficient to compensate talented employees and to pay for all the development activities discussed. Without profit, that is, without funds above those needed to pay salaries and overhead, developmental activity slows and your firm can stagnate.

All employees must accept those goals as a valued norm. Saying "we must be profitable" can cause staff to behave that way. Yet, in many firms, profitability is *not* a value.

> Herein lies one of the greatest fallacies that design firms harbor about excellence—that excellence and profitability are not necessarily compatible.

Profitability is *essential* to excellence in your design firm.

One of the better long-range plans belongs to O'Brien-Gere Engineering. In one of its five-year plans, the firm's leaders decided that they never really wanted O'Brien-Gere Engineering to be a 2,000-person firm. They did feel the need to aim for six to eight percent growth, in order to provide upward mobility for the staff. If the firm were to stagnate, it could lose some key people.

So, managers developed a plan for growth. Along with growth in size they set monetary growth goals, to pay for the increased number of people. And their marketing targets grew accordingly. They made a conscious decision about what they wanted the firm to become, and what rate of growth would be needed to ensure that the firm would be a healthy place.

The firm has several divisions, each headed by a vice president. A lot of pressure existed for each of the vice presidents to produce the desired profit. One division was not to subsidize another.

If some employees or divisions do not accept the belief in profitability, as a standard, the person or group that does not reach its goal can antagonize the person or group that does. The beliefs must be shared throughout your firm.

Economic growth and profitability are values that all of your employees need to accept.

The seven common beliefs discussed in this chapter do not necessarily have to be *your* personal or even your firm-wide values. In fact, you may disagree with some. They're *examples*. But your values, whatever they are, do have to be *shared* in your firm to gain the excellence that comes from shared pursuit. Your firm's energy will be better focused and directed toward action when it shares your values and your sense of mission.

Talk within your firm about the values that you want your firm to have and how you can *communicate* these values to your employees, so that everyone accepts them and follows them on a day-to-day basis.

The persistence of a firm's principals in keeping an eye on the firm's values, and in guiding the daily activities of the staff so that they are consistent with those values, is prerequisite to achieving excellence.

CHAPTER 7

IMPLEMENTING EXCELLENCE

In the previous six chapters, you've read about scores of ways in which design and engineering firms have sparked greater excellence for themselves. Now it's time to put those ideas to work in *your* firm.

This chapter is composed of twenty questions. They give practical substance to concepts that have been discussed throughout this book.

> Each question comes with a worksheet to fill in—a tool that functions as a clarifier and a plan for action.

By developing your own responses to each worksheet, you will, almost automatically, start your firm on the path to greater excellence—one solid step at a time.

Each question is posed on a separate page or page spread. There is a developmental sequence to the questions; some must precede others. However, the sequence does not absolutely parallel the order in which the ideas have been presented in the book. That's intentional.

- Complete the 20 worksheets
- Follow the instructions on the worksheets: Work on
  them as a firm, in small groups, or individually

In a firm of three or five or seven people, get together in a single group. In larger firms, work in subgroups of three to five members. Treat this project as a collateral activity, as discussed in Chapter 1. You can't shut off your production time, but you can take an hour or two beyond regular working hours. At each meeting, focus on just *one* of these worksheets.

If working in subgroups, have each subgroup appoint one person to meet with representatives of other subgroups—three to five at a time. If you have groups of five, your second level represents 25 people. Your third level represents 125 people. And, as those representatives come together, you can hear from 625 people with no more than four consecutive meetings. With only five levels, even the largest firms can be accommodated.

> The goal is for *everyone* in your firm to become personally involved with the worksheets and with the planning of your firm's future.

Each worksheet features actions to take, steps you can do tomorrow or over the next two weeks or two months or two years. Each checklist forces you to ask these questions:

- *What* is the action that needs to happen
- *How* are we going to achieve the change we want
- *When* should we achieve results
- *Who* should be responsible for seeing that the
  change takes place

Many worksheets have a built-in review process. You'll need reminders to prevent you from falling back into the ways you've been doing things.

If you commit to doing something within a specific time frame, you're more likely to achieve the increments you're seeking. That's why many of the worksheets have target dates incorporated into them.

Start now. Begin with the first question and go right on through to the last one.

- You'll begin to sense a flow of progress
- You'll begin to experience the satisfaction that comes
  from integrating the ideal of excellence with the
  practical advantages of better management and marketing

1. WHAT ARE OUR STRONGEST VALUES?

Construct a list of your firm's strongest values—qualities which are *specific to your firm* and which separate, or differentiate, your firm from others.

Be careful not to list general "motherhood" statements; they won't provide useful guidance for action.

What do we value, uniquely, as a firm?	What specific steps can we take to enhance that value?	By when?	How will we know when we have achieved this value?
1. *example* Consistently high quality design	1. Design reviews and critiques by all interested firm members at key decision points. 2. Occupancy visits by all interested firm members of all completed projects, seeking refinements that could have improved the project.	March 1	Questionnaire rating firm's perceived design excellence, completed now and 18 months from now (to measure progress). Test both employees and clients.
2.			
3.			
4.			

2. WHAT SHOULD OUR NICHE BE?

The worksheet below will help you to define your firm's niche and to plan actions that will make the most of that niche.

It is important to differentiate between things your firm does that *few or no other* firms can do and parts of your practice that are "me too" (such as proofing specifications and shop drawings).

Ask yourselves if you serve a special market or group of clients; if you provide special services or unique skills; if you serve a special locale or region; and if you operate your practice in a unique way.

What are our niches?	What action can we take to best take advantage of our uniqueness?	By when?	By whom?	How will we know when we've achieved the result?
1. *example* Adaptive re-use of mid-size commercial structures	Find site, restore, and move our office into a historic building	Complete purchase within 4 months; occupancy within 2 years	David S. will lead effort	Deed or title; occupancy
2.				
3.				
4.				

3. WHAT SHOULD WE DO ABOUT SUBGROUPS?

Subgroups in many firms center around a technical discipline or specialty. For firm excellence, they should also be organized around a service, or set of services, for a specific type of client.

---

1. Would our firm benefit from having subgroups?

_____ Yes   _____ No

2. If yes, what service or client type should we focus on?

example Develop spec housing

_____

_____

_____

3. How will we maintain fluidity and open communication between subgroups?

example No one can spend more than 80 percent time in any one group. No one can remain in any subgroup longer than 18 months.

_____

_____

_____

_____

---

4. HOW CAN WE BETTER LISTEN TO OUR CLIENTS?

New ideas require *acceptance* in your marketplace. You won't have that acceptance unless you're in close touch with your clients.

What actions can we take to gather more information from our clients and/or users about their problems or unfulfilled needs?	Who will implement the action?	By when?	How will we use the information we gather?	How will we evaluate the success of our actions?
1. *example* Every client will be interviewed at project quarter points by someone not working on the project to identify best and worst features of our performance and to get a client performance rating	Stan R.	2 months	Information will be presented at a briefing to refine our approach	Changes in client ratings of our performance
2.				
3.				
4.				

5. HOW CAN WE STRENGTHEN OUR CORE SKILLS?

What should your "core" skills be? You must have a common denominator that underlies *all* of your firm's activities and services. Your core skills are the base or trunk from which everything else grows and branches.

What are our core skills?	What actions can we take to ensure the strength of our core skills?	By whom?	By when?	How will we know we've achieved or maintained our desired level of strength?
1. *example* Geotechnical expertise	Identify biggest soil-caused problems	Art B.	3 months	New work will be aligned to areas of greatest need.
2.				
3.				
4.				

What new opportunities could grow from the core skill?	In sequencing new opportunity areas, which should go first, second, etc.?	What can we do to encourage growth of the new area?	By whom?	By when?	How will we know when we've integrated the new area?
1. *example* Continuing services for structures that have problems over time	3rd	Offer preventive maintenance program to top 10 clients with the need	Art B.	5 months	Count percentage of projects under continuing contracts.
2.					
3.					
4.					

6. HOW CAN WE KEEP OUR PRINCIPALS IN THE FIELD?

While your livelihood depends on day-to-day productivity in delivering to clients what you've promised them, your principals must also maintain a longer-term perspective and a sensitivity to the marketplace. This they can do only if they are regularly in the field.

What actions can we take to keep our principal(s) in the field with clients, users, and staff?	By whom?	By when?	How will we know that we've achieved successful results?
1. *example* Each principal will participate in one focus group per month, discussing trends in that month's category	Ted W.	3 months	Measure changes in the firm that grow out of ideas from the discussions
2.			
3.			
4.			

7. HOW WILL WE ENSURE INNOVATION IN OUR FIRM?

Experimentation is essential to innovation. List areas in your firm that would benefit from new ideas and plan for support of experiments.

Areas in our firm that would benefit from new ideas	What can we do to promote new ideas in that area?	By whom?	How will we support that person?	How will we know if we've been successful?
In Design:				
In Production:				
In Management: *example* Firm-wide automation	Form an automation triad that seeks new opportunities	Lee K.	Budget 2 hours per week release time	Internal survey of managerial effectiveness (before/after automation)
In Financial Management:				
In Marketing:				

8. WHAT CAN WE DO TO ENSURE COLLATERAL ACTIVITY?

One of the keys to nurturing new ideas and approaches is through an environment in which small groups can gather to experiment—in a collateral mode that is free from day-to-day pressures of productivity needs and deadlines.

1. How can we create opportunities for individuals or small groups to experiment with new ideas and processes?

_____

_____

_____

_____

2. What can we do to keep production pressures away from experimenters?

_____

_____

_____

_____

3. What incentives can we build in to encourage experimentation?

_____

_____

_____

_____

9. HOW CAN WE PUT OUR FIRM INTO AN ACTION MODE?

Improvement in your firm can only come through the testing of new ideas on a regular basis. That requires *action*, not deliberation. See what you can do to increase your propensity to "try it."

---

1. How can we increase informal and continuous interchange between principal(s) and staff?

_____

_____

2. What issues can be assigned to temporary task groups? List in sequence.

a. _____

b. _____

c. _____

3. How can we create autonomy for firm members to enable them to carry through on ideas of their own—without risk of penalty?

_____

_____

4. How can we increase the quantity of small tests, experiments, and changes?

_____

_____

5. How can we get clients to participate in our tests?

_____

_____

6. How will we spread good new ideas through our firm?

_____

_____

10. WHAT CAN WE DO TO ACHIEVE EXCELLENT COMMUNICATION?

A common trait of excellent firms is communication that is continuous, open, informal, and intense.

1. How can we increase the amount of informal communication in our firm, especially from top to bottom, and bottom to top?

a. _____

b. _____

c. _____

2. How can we facilitate greater frankness and openness, so that even a junior staff person will argue his or her convictions with principals?

a. _____

b. _____

c. _____

3. What steps can we take to modify our offices to facilitate and support more intense and ongoing communication? (Closer proximity? Chalkboards? Flip charts?)

a. _____

b. _____

c. _____

4. What organized programs or events can we create to regularly facilitate open communication and new ideas? (Annual retreat with a communication consultant?)

a. _____

b. _____

c. _____

11. WHAT SHOULD WE DO TO REMIND US OF OUR VALUES?

Having visible models or notices is one way to create positive stimulae and reminders of behaviors you'd like to have happen in your firm.

What are 20 actions that staff in our firm should take to further our firm's values?	What kind of "sign" would provide reminders and encouragement?	Where posted?	By whom?	How will we know we've been successful?
1. *example* Dress in such a way as to reflect the firm's value of beauty	"Look as sharp as you'd like your work to be"	Office entry	Chris P.	Internal and external notice
2.				
3.				
4.				

12. HOW CAN WE ENCOURAGE INNOVATORS?

For an experimenting climate to thrive, support must be created for people in the firm who pursue and "champion" new ideas.

---

1. What steps can we take to encourage people to pioneer in sponsoring new ideas and developments?

a. _____

b. _____

c. _____

2. What can we do to increase the *number* of new ideas or experiments in our firm?

a. _____

b. _____

c. _____

3. How can we shield experimenters from being consumed by production work?

a. _____

b. _____

c. _____

4. How can we use other firm members, such as senior or founding people, as examples of innovation?

a. _____

b. _____

c. _____

5. How can we use internal competition to spark enthusiasm for new idea development?

a. _____

b. _____

c. _____

---

13. HOW CAN WE SUPPORT GROWTH OF OUR OWN PEOPLE?

One common denominator of all excellent firms is their commitment to developing in-house talent. Commitment *to* people breeds commitment *from* them—and greater productivity.

1. How can we systematically achieve face-to-face communication with our staff, to listen for their needs and to create training ideas?

a. _____

b. _____

c. _____

2. What steps would be best for our firm to organize a training and career development program?

a. _____

b. _____

c. _____

3. What steps can we take in making job assignments that will encourage people to best use their new training?

a. _____

b. _____

c. _____

4. In what ways can new skills and increased productivity be tied to increased job security?

a. _____

b. _____

c. _____

5. What incentives can we create that will contribute to desire for greater productivity and more training?

a. _____

b. _____

c. _____

14. HOW CAN WE REWARD OUR PEOPLE?

Recognition for achievement of desired performance is very important to prompting greater excellence throughout your firm.

Area of Achievement	What recognition or awards are most appropriate for excellent performance?	What frequency of recognition is most appropriate?	Who decides or confers the recognition?	By when will the award be initiated?
In Design:				
In Production:				
In Management:				
In Financial Management:				
In Marketing: *example* New business	Cup for outstanding performance—rotating	Annual	Glorya H.	September 1

15. WHAT CAN WE DO TO CREATE A SENSE OF BELONGING?

Excellent firms are more than "a place to work." They engender a sense of belonging and sometimes a sense of extended family.

What activities can our firm undertake to heighten the individual's sense of belonging?	What action can we take to implement this activity?	Who will develop this activity?	By when?	How will we know this has been achieved?
1. *example* Solicit news of family and out-of-office activities for in-house broadside	Designate news collector and column writer	Victoria C-C.	Bimonthly, beginning October 1	Increased sharing of personal news; positive comments on column
2.				
3.				
4.				

16. HOW CAN WE FUNCTION WITH A SMALL CENTRAL STAFF?

[This worksheet is for larger firms that employ people to coordinate sub-groups or branch offices, to provide firm-wide common support, to manage finances, or to establish personnel guidelines.]

1. How lean can we keep our coordinating central staff?

_____

_____

2. What is the absolute minimum number of staff people we need to get by in different areas?

Function	Minimum staff needed	Reason
example Public relations	One-fourth of one person	Can use outside freelance consultants as needs arise

3. What functions can be reassigned to operating groups?

a. *example* Professional development training will be planned by each project manager

b. _____

c. _____

4. Which tasks can be simplified?

a. *example* All time sheets and project reporting will be automated

b. _____

c. _____

5. Which multiple functions can be combined and handled by one person?

a. *example* All financial matters will be managed by Sari K.

b. _____

c. _____

17. HOW CAN I MAKE A VALUED CONTRIBUTION?

[A copy of this worksheet should be completed by each person in the firm.]

Job title	What are my primary responsibilities?	How can each of my responsibilities be carried out to reflect, more directly, my firm's values?
1. *example* Secretary	Typing firm's correspondence	Develop a letterhead with type style that reflects the historic preservation emphasis of the firm
2.		
3.		
4.		

18. HOW CAN WE PERFECT WHAT WE'RE DOING?

A prerequisite for all excellent firms is quality obsession. But perfection comes a step at a time. Identify incremental, bite-sized steps you can take in different areas of your firm to perfect how you're currently performing.

Aspects of our firm	What steps can be tried to further perfect current performance?	By whom?	By when?	How will we measure success?
In Design:				
In Production:				
In Management:				
In Financial Management: *example* Tracking of actual project costs	Acquire integrated software for CADD system	Areta B.	6 months	Realize more accurate future estimates

19. WHAT ARE EXCELLENCE-BUILDING BEHAVIORS IN LEADERS?

[This worksheet is to be completed by the principal or firm's leader.] Values are wonderful to articulate and to share as a firm. But how will you ensure that you behave consistently with your stated values?

---

1. How can I, as a leader in my firm, constantly remind myself of the firm's values?

_____

_____

_____

2. What should I do to continuously remind others of the firm's values and goals?

a. _____

b. _____

c. _____

d. _____

3. In what ways can I share information about what's happening in the firm and about progress in performing consistently with our values?

a. _____

b. _____

c. _____

d. _____

4. What can I do to spark a greater degree of fun in the firm?

_____

_____

_____

_____

---

20. WHAT CAN WE DO TO FULLY COMMUNICATE OUR MISSION?

The previous 19 questions—each in its own way—have helped define your firm and its mission.

The most important information a firm has to share is what its mission is. The more people know about something, the more they tend to care about it, support it, and communicate it to the marketplace.

---

1. How can our firm's overall objectives be shared and discussed, so that everyone knows where we're going?

_____

_____

2. How should new employees be informed of the firm's mission?

_____

_____

3. In what ways can an increasing amount of information about the firm be shared by an increasing number of people?

_____

_____

4. How can each project be performed consistently without total mission?

_____

_____

5. How will we know if everyone in our firm is fully informed of and cares about the firm's objectives?

_____

_____
